Get a Grip

Anxiety

From Understanding to Combating.

From Shakes & Shivers to Confidence & Contentment.

Understand It, Own It, Smash It!

S A Nightingale

IQRA PUBLISHING LTD

READ·HEAL·LEAD

TABLE OF CONTENTS

FREE GIFT JUST FOR YOU

My Miss Worry,
You don't know how much you mean to me ...
Words cannot express my feelings, no matter how much I try!
All I can say is that you are my little world, the coolness of my eyes, a
part of me ...
Thank you for coming into my life and becoming a part of my family.
*I wish to see you not as a worrier but as a **Warrior**; become the **Master***
of this monster!
So, reframe your overthinking behind that train of unstoppable thoughts

...

And when you find yourself trapped in a whirlwind of negative self-talk,
offload those negative emotions in Prostration ...
Have faith!
Always remember, prayers do come true.
Here is a book I dedicate to you, my sweetheart.
So, Get a Grip!

Love You Always ...

Yours only,
Miss Nightingale

S A Nightingale

AN INTRODUCTION TO ANXIETY

 "There is only one way to happiness and that is to cease worrying about things which are beyond the power of our will."

— EPICTETUS

Anxiety can be a terrifying and overwhelming experience, especially if it's something you're unfamiliar with or do not understand. For a long time, people have been afraid to talk about their anxiety for fear that it paints them in a negative or bad light to those around them. Thankfully, however, the discussion has been opened, and more and more people are finding the courage to speak up about this mental health condition.

As a licensed dentist, I am well aware of anxiety in one particular aspect: dentistry. I've chosen to write this book, along with the guidance of my husband, a licensed psychiatrist, so that others can resolve their past traumas and find solutions to their anxiety symptoms without delay.

I've also wanted to write a book about anxiety specifically because of my dear friend, a lady I endearingly call Miss Worry. My friend's experience with anxiety was quite meaningful, as it helped me to see people from a different perspective. I now understand them better, so when they talk to me, I can understand and feel their struggles. I also now recognize that sometimes, when a person appears to be toxic, it might already be a cry for help. Just as I helped my friend overcome anxiety with lots of love and encouragement, I want to help others with this book. I want you and all my readers to know that you are not alone, that it is not your fault you have this condition, and that you can talk about it and get help. I hope this book can serve as a guide to you in understanding and helping others who are dealing with anxiety.

Let's talk about Natasha and her private struggles with dentistry anxiety, plus how she learned to finally move on.

When Natasha was a young girl of about six years, she had to see a dentist to remove a troublesome baby tooth. Not knowing what to expect, the event already caused a slight bit of discomfort. Once Natasha was in the office, however, the dentist asked her mother to leave the room during the procedure. Being alone during such a new and uneasy experience is scary enough, but with the sounds and sights of the dentist office added in, Natasha felt completely afraid.

Over the years, Natasha went to great lengths to avoid visiting the dentist, only seeking help when she was in terrible pain. She wasn't getting the care she needed to prevent further problems, which even worsened her experiences. Each time she needed treatment, it entailed drilling, extraction, and disappointing results. Natasha went from doctor to doctor to find a place—and a professional—who would take the time to understand. Many of them were less considerate of her now that she was an adult.

Until she came to me.

I understand that anxiety is a natural response and that we all feel it throughout our lives. Natasha went through a traumatic experience as a child, shaping the way she viewed dentistry for the rest of her life. I'm so glad she opened up to me about her anxiety because she and I were able to create a plan that has given her the results and care she has long needed. Not just for her dental health but also for her anxiety related to dental procedures.

Now when she visits, we use coping mechanisms, such as a stress ball to allow her to relieve the tension she feels in the moment, as well as headphones to block out the noise and keep her mind from forming those worrisome thoughts that help to fuel her anxieties.

Natasha needed emotional support more than anything, which is the main reason I am writing this book for you. Many people are afraid to talk about anxiety for fear of being looked down on. Some see it as a weakness, and so we hide our flaws and pretend like everything is okay. But, as we have just discussed, it prevents people from getting the help they need to avoid bigger issues. In Natasha's situation, she could have had the preventative cleanings and care to keep her from the heavier, more invasive treatments that came later if she had gotten proper help for her anxiety.

Throughout this book, we will go through the various types of anxiety, including one specific form that affects nearly 60% of the population. You'll learn to master the monster within, hushing those thoughts as you discover proven techniques to improve your life today. We'll hear about celebrities and their struggles, and also how they have overcome their fears and worked toward living their lives to the fullest. Even if you aren't sure what you're experiencing is anxiety, this book will help you learn the clear signs of a panic attack, as well as simple, useful tools you can find in your own home to resolve your symptoms quickly.

So, please join me as we venture into the beginning of this book, where we will start to discuss anxiety on a basic level. Here we will gain a better understanding of what anxiety does in our daily lives and how we can finally start coping with our symptoms so that our lives can improve immediately.

What I want for you more than anything else is to feel comfortable with who you are—anxiety and all. Life is a joyous creation we should all find wonder and excitement in, and we can do that even when facing our toughest of times. Learning to love ourselves and accept who we are is the first step in finding solutions and cures to the things that ail us. I want to see you find ultimate happiness in your life as you resolve your fears and stresses and reduce your anxiety. Let's begin!

CHAPTER 1

THE MONSTER WITHIN: GETTING TO KNOW
MORE ABOUT ANXIETY

Anxiety is one of the most common mental illnesses in the United States. Because of this, you can find solace in knowing that you're not alone in your troubles with fear. Many people of different ages and backgrounds face anxiety every day. Let's review the facts and numbers to see just how prevalent anxiety is.

- Anxiety disorders are the most common mental illness in the U.S, affecting 40 million adults in the United States aged 18 and older, or 18.1% of the population every year.
- Anxiety disorders are highly treatable, yet only 36.9% of those suffering receive treatment.
- People with an anxiety disorder are three to five times more likely to go to the doctor and six times more likely to be hospitalized for psychiatric disorders than those who do not suffer from anxiety disorders.
- Generalized anxiety disorder (GAD) is the most common anxiety disorder among older adults, although anxiety

disorders in this population are frequently associated with traumatic events such as a fall or acute illness.

At first glance, it might be hard to believe this. Some people you have met throughout your life might appear as though they have everything in their life together. People like that often have all the answers and are happy every time you see them. This, however, doesn't mean that their lives are perfect. As we've already discussed, everyone has fears and things that stress them out, and those two things can lead to anxiety in people you would least expect.

It has taken a lot of courage for people to begin the discussion of anxiety because no matter what we do, we are always trying to look our best and behave as though we believe others expect us to. This can make living with anxiety very difficult at times because the very nature of anxiety means that we are lost in our minds, drowning in thoughts we wish we weren't having. This also means that we are occupied and unable to stay present in our current situation, which can often make us behave in ways we do not like. These behaviors, such as tapping your foot, biting your nails, or other nervous antics, are the unwanted symptoms that accompany anxiety. They cause us to look at ourselves with an even finer magnifying glass than before, criticizing ourselves and what we are doing as though we have been misbehaving.

This is the first problem with anxiety. It turns into a cycle that we struggle to escape from. It begins with a thought causing us to dwell on a fear that isn't truly present. Once the fear takes hold and the thoughts continue coming in, we find ourselves displaying physical symptoms that then make us feel regretful and embarrassed. Trying to hide these symptoms and our true anxiety can make us feel even more alone. Because of this, we may withdraw from our friends and family instead of seeking their help.

I'm here to tell you that the people around you want to help you more than you will ever know. There are people in your life who truly love you and care for you, and they want to see you feel better as you grow and heal from your fears. It's important to know that you are not alone in this struggle and that there is nothing wrong with who you are. Having anxiety is a normal part of being human, and the sooner you accept that and accept yourself for who you are, the sooner you can begin to feel better and move past your anxiety.

WHAT EXACTLY IS ANXIETY?

According to the American Psychological Association, "Anxiety is an emotion characterized by feelings of tension, worried thoughts, and physical changes like increased blood pressure." This means that for every thought we have involving anxiety, such as fear and worry, our physical bodies begin to display changes that will make us feel even further uncomfortable. Sometimes these feelings can arise from traumas in our past, making us connect certain things that are otherwise non-life-threatening with the fear for survival.

The Anxiety and Depression Association of America goes on to explain anxiety as a ". . . real, serious medical condition." They explain anxiety as one of the more common mental disorders that can become highly pervasive in our daily lives. Even though anxiety comes with life, and it is completely normal to experience a little bit of anxiety from time to time, it can become overwhelming and detrimental to the many aspects of our lives if it shows up persistently. Anxiety can cause dread and dismay, overshadowing events that may have once caused great joy.

The American Psychiatric Association explains anxiety as ". . . a normal reaction to stress." Of course, when our stress overwhelms us and leads to unwanted thoughts and behaviors, anxiety can take hold and begin to affect more of our lives. Anxiety can have an impact on things as simple as grocery shopping, just as it can cause difficulties in relationships and career choices. Anxiety is known to force people to avoid certain situations that may increase their symptoms, and this can lead to more anxiety as the person becomes isolated and falls deeper into their fears.

It's important to understand that even though anxiety can be difficult to overcome, many treatments are available. With everything from alternative remedies to cognitive behavioral therapy, relief from anxiety is closer than most people might realize. Later in this book, we will go over those treatments in depth so that you have all the tools required to heal from the inside out and move forward with your life.

WHAT DOES AN ANXIETY ATTACK FEEL LIKE?

For Aleena, a young woman dealing with general anxiety disorder, anxiety has become a living nightmare. She says that when her anxiety creeps up on her, she feels like she cannot catch her breath or control her thoughts.

Once, while waiting in line at a beauty salon, Aleena started to feel anxiety because she knew she'd be put on the spot. Even though having her hair done was something she looked forward to, sitting in the reception area waiting for her name to be called only made her fearful and jittery. She felt like everyone would be watching her, ridiculing her for even the smallest things. That, to her, is exactly what anxiety is—worrying over the simplest ideas for so long that they start to feel enormous. She felt worried and frightened, and the otherwise wonderful experience gave her body aches for days afterward.

For Gia, anxiety is like waking up each morning and wishing she hadn't. Her dread follows her everywhere, making her feel sick and jittery. It's an endless rollercoaster ride, taking her up and down so quickly that she might just throw up.

Anxiety can also come on suddenly without any reason at all. Rosie explains it as a feeling that hits her hard, like a massive wave. She gets overwhelmed with that sense of doom, the one that makes us feel like something terrible will indeed happen. She has to force herself to breathe, but even then, her anxiety continues. She can't catch her breath; she sweats and loses focus. Even though she's not in any danger, her anxiety is trying very hard to convince her otherwise.

Anxiety is different for everyone, but we can all agree that it is tremendously horrible to feel.

So, how exactly does anxiety impact our bodies and our minds as we go about our daily lives? What types of symptoms are we likely to experience, and which ones have you maybe not caught or noticed?

Sometimes we experience anxiety to a very small degree, making us believe that it's not a problem and that we have it under control. You might even experience flare-ups from time to time, feeling the full weight of your fears and anxiety for an extended period. Even if you believe you have things handled and are living your life to the fullest, there's a good chance you might still be in need of help. If your anxiety is enough to make you stay away from certain situations for fear of feeling that panic, then it's time to review those symptoms to know whether or not you are taking complete control over your life. Remember, we all have the right to be happy and do the things that bring us joy, and we should never let anxiety stand in the way.

For starters, we must understand that an anxiety attack is techni-cally a panic attack, and it involves excessive fearful thoughts that leave you feeling worried and scared that things will not turn out the way you wish they could be. This moment of panic can last for a few minutes or a few hours, depending on how big of a fear you are dealing with. The good news is that over time you can easily reduce your symptoms and shorten the amount of anxiety you deal with on a daily basis. As we've discussed, it is normal to expe-rience anxiety, and therefore you must first accept the fact that you will never completely get rid of anxiety. In a later chapter, we will discuss the benefits of good anxiety and how it helps us manage certain situations in our lives. Our main goal in this book is to get to a point where we can accept our anxiety for what it is and allow it to help us rather than hinder us.

Let's begin by identifying some of the symptoms involved in an anxiety attack so that you can be aware of what it is you're experi-encing rather than being afraid of what is happening to you. In any situation, we are always fearful to experience something we do not understand. When we know more about the things that are impacting us, such as anxiety, then we can approach the situation well informed and ready to find a solution.

THE PHYSICAL SYMPTOMS OF ANXIETY

When we are talking about the physical symptoms involved in an anxiety attack, we basically are recognizing the things anxiety has done to our physical bodies that are often noticeable by others. These things can make us feel uncomfortable about who we are and how we are behaving, and after having the symptoms of anxi-ety, we may be left feeling embarrassed or shameful.

One of the most common symptoms of anxiety involves twitching or shaking. Depending on the amount of stress or fear you are experiencing, you may find yourself being a little jittery, or you might notice you're trembling heavily enough to want to completely escape the situation and be left alone. I know this feeling all too well. Like so many others, I personally have difficulties in social situations where there are many people involved and a lot going on around me. Even before arriving at the event, and maybe even as early as hearing about it and needing to prepare, I will feel those anxious trembles kicking in.

Needless to say, by the time I experienced the main event, I was full of anxiety and felt nothing like myself. This obvious symptom can make you feel as if people are watching you and judging how you are acting when, in fact, it isn't the case at all. This is where anxiety can be crushing to our self-esteem and our overall confidence. Thanks to some wonderful techniques that I will share later in this book, I've been able to move past this type of anxiety and learn to accept it for what it is as I heal from the fears that were causing it. And I'm here to do the same for you.

Aside from the trembles, anxiety can also cause dryness in our mouths, fast and shallow breathing, and feeling as though we are exhausted or weakened. These different symptoms go hand in hand as the thoughts and fears driving our anxiety take hold. Typically it begins with a rush of adrenaline, the very thing our bodies are designed to use in a situation when we feel the need to run away or face the threat head-on. This is part of our natural physiology and can also help us in a good way, something we will touch on later in this book. Basically, adrenaline fuels our bodies to help us escape a situation where we feel threatened, or it helps us strengthen our defenses so that we can fight and protect ourselves.

The adrenaline we feel causes our hearts to beat faster and our breathing to become more rapid. With faster breathing and a heightened sense of awareness, our mouths dry out, and our palms get sweaty, all while we are facing our fears in our minds.

THE PSYCHOLOGICAL SYMPTOMS OF ANXIETY

As our bodies go through these physical symptoms, our minds are constantly battling to regain peace and resolve stress. The mind is a very powerful thing, and it can have us believe things that are not true. As much as our fears are often rooted in fact, it is our worrisome minds that ask the question: What if?

What if that were me?
What if I forgot to turn the oven off?
What if there are bacteria on the door handle?

These questions that we ask ourselves fuel our deepest fears and cause us to dwell on things that don't deserve our attention. Worrying about things that are out of our control only steals precious time away from the things that matter most to us. And those things, such as our family and friends, the hobbies that we love, and the places we long to see, suffer as we drift further into our fears and anxiety.

During an anxiety attack, it's common for us to lose our focus and become unable to concentrate on the things that are most important. This might also be recognized as brain fog, although that typically involves a general sense of feeling detached. Being unable to concentrate and focus due to anxiety means that we are lost in our fearful thoughts and unable to bring ourselves back to the present reality. Those dreaded fears have taken hold, and the best thing we can do is recognize this as soon as it happens and stop them before they run away.

Aside from concentration, our behaviors can also suffer on a mental level. It is common to become irritable and moody when faced with fearful situations. Typically, as an anxiety attack begins to take hold, and even well after it is over, we feel little like ourselves. It becomes very hard to get back into the groove of things and feel like we have control over our lives. When these feelings of inadequacy, embarrassment, and shame come on, we are left feeling angry and upset. Unfortunately, we tend to take out our feelings on others even when we try very hard not to. This is one reason why anxiety is so detrimental to not only the person involved but also the people in their lives. When a person suffers from a mental illness, so too do the others surrounding them.

WHAT HAPPENS TO US AFTER THE ATTACK?

Recovering from an anxiety attack can take some time, depending on how long it lasted. It may also matter as to what type of fear you've experienced and how heavy a toll it took on your emotional state. This is why discovering your triggers and recognizing an anxiety attack as soon as possible can help you overcome the fears and stresses involved, as well as heal from the symptoms as quickly as possible.

After experiencing anxiety, you might notice you aren't sleeping as well, and you may even be dealing with insomnia, where it is difficult for you to fall asleep at all. Lying in bed alone at night can be difficult when you are trying to process thoughts that you have not yet resolved. Those same thoughts are the ones that can fuel your anxiety attacks and lead to more mental and physical symptoms down the road.

Because of the lack of sleep, or even just because you're having difficulty relaxing at times, you may begin to feel exhausted or weakened. This can lead to additional mood swings, and it can also make you feel restless inside. When we are unable to sleep properly, our bodies and minds are unable to repair themselves from the trauma that came from that day. This is why sleep is so crucial. Having the right amount of sleep for the activities you do helps your mind to repair cells and rejuvenate the physical body. On the other hand, stress only degrades those cells and impairs the healing process.

WHAT CAN BE DONE?

It might seem like anxiety is nothing more than a vicious cycle that is impossible to escape. With one thing leading to the next, you might be asking yourself: How do I ever get off of this circus ride? Well, seeking out the information in this book alone is proof that you are willing to break the mold and do what is necessary to resolve your fears and get your stress in check. It's not an easy process, but just like me, you are willing to do the work and improve your life for the better.

There are ways that you can help to minimize your anxiety attacks to the point where they are truly under control. With different types of therapy and medications, and also by using the support of your friends and family, anxiety can become more normal and acceptable in your life.

Truly understanding anxiety and where it comes from is our first step in handling an attack. The second step is to identify your triggers and learn what it is that may be causing you the most fear or stress in your life.

It might be difficult digging deep to better understand yourself, but it is all part of the journey we will do together.

WHAT CAUSES ANXIETY?

While we already know that anxiety can come from natural factors that our human bodies are designed to handle, such as the rush of adrenaline that we get from facing dangerous situations, there are also other factors that can play into why a person becomes anxious. Of these different factors, we find that the environment, things we consume, and genetics have the biggest impact.

In our environments, which include the place we live, the work we do, and the hobbies we keep, we routinely face stress and fear. Our environment is the core of our physical world, and it can help shape us into who we are because it builds the setting of our lives. With everything from our relationships to the places we frequent, our environments can bring on a diverse range of stressors that can be hard to navigate when you're unsure of how you feel and the emotions you're having in any given moment. This is, yet again, why it is so important to understand yourself and know your limits before you can begin to find solutions and treatments that work best for you.

Aside from the environment, the different substances we use can impact our mental health regularly. With everything from food choices to medications, we can experience a diverse range of feelings and emotions that impact the way we perceive the world around us. For example, caffeine is a well-known stimulant that can create feelings of anxiousness, especially if you're already dealing with fears and stresses. Aside from that, certain prescription medications can have adverse effects and create feelings of anxiety and depression. There are other substances as well, such as food additives, stimulants, and both genetically modified ingredients, as well as substances that have been given additional hormones to increase growth. Truly, nature has provided us with the best medicine of all, and that is wholesome, healthy foods grown organically. Whenever I feel as though I am not myself, I start with this first, as it is something I am putting into my body throughout the day, every single day of the week.

Finally, genetics can play a major role in whether or not a person is prone to anxiety. It is believed that mental illnesses run in families and that if you have a relative with a mental illness, the chances of you yourself being diagnosed are a little higher. There are many factors involved in this concept because it isn't only genetics that can impact your mental health but also the various other factors that we've discussed.

Even after all this, sometimes you can't find a reason as to why anxiety has impacted you and your life. Some people experience anxiety seemingly out of nowhere, and it is those times that can be the most difficult to understand and make sense of. Let's take a closer look at a personal story to better understand this form of anxiety and how someone with it can find relief.

A Personal Story

People everywhere deal with anxiety, including famous people that often look like they have it all together. Sometimes the anxiety these people face has no true reasoning, but it is just there lingering in the background, growing until it impacts a moment that becomes unforgettable.

Actress and mental health advocate Mara Wilson is one of these people. As a child actor, Mara was routinely immersed in a world of busyness, fame, and high demand in an often unforgiving industry. Despite these, Mara has said that her anxiety is a part of who she is and that she would not be herself without it.

Finding a solution to her panic attacks, Mara has made use of various workbooks and breathing exercises to bring herself to the present and work through the anxiety that may be dampening any given situation. In addition, she uses the simple 3–3–3 technique to bring herself out of her mind and into the present surroundings. By listing off three items she can see, three she can hear, and three she can feel, Mara is able to slip away from the thoughts that are causing her dread and arrive into the present world where we would all like to remain.

Mara remains focused on learning to set boundaries and creating a structure that can help alleviate stress and fear. But aside from this, she knows it is important to forgive yourself when you go through something difficult and be compassionate about what you are going through—just as you would for someone else. Sometimes it is our own actions that can cause more fear and stress in our lives. We must learn to be kind to ourselves so that we may grow and heal.

WHAT HAVE WE LEARNED?

Throughout this chapter, we've found that anxiety is a heavy weight to carry, and we all carry it differently.

- Anxiety begins in the mind and manifests in the body.
- Many of the symptoms involved can make our fears worse as we believe something terrible is truly happening to us.
- Anxiety can be caused by our genes and also our environments. Sometimes we have anxiety for no apparent reason.
- Treatments are everywhere, but the first step is to acknowledge that you're not feeling like yourself and need help.

WHAT IS YOUR CURRENT ANXIETY LEVEL?

Use the following quiz, which was modeled after the Depression and Anxiety Self-assessment Quiz, to help yourself identify how stressed and anxious you truly are. Be honest about your answers, then use this assessment to speak with a professional for treatment options.

1. Are you feeling down or less interested in the things that once brought you joy?
2. Do you have trouble falling asleep, staying asleep, or remaining motivated and productive throughout your day?
3. Have you had difficulty eating, or have you felt nauseous recently?
4. Do you feel nervous, restless, or fidgety?
5. Do you notice yourself feeling irritable, easily annoyed, or otherwise unable to relax?

6. Do you fear that something terrible will happen to you or those you care about?
7. Have you experienced a panic attack?

If you were able to answer yes to even a couple of these questions, you should speak with your healthcare provider. If you answered more than half, you are most likely experiencing anxiety and should speak to someone to find a treatment to help ease your symptoms.

MOVING AHEAD

Now that we understand anxiety and recognize the various symptoms accompanying a panic attack, we can focus more on the two different sides of anxiety. Just like most things in life, anxiety comes with both good and bad contributions. We've hinted at a few of those here when discussing why anxiety happens and the impact it has on our bodies, both physically and mentally.

It is never easy addressing our flaws and coming to terms with who we truly are. I've felt the pressures of needing to be "normal" or "perfect" in many situations, both in my personal life and in my career. You must not forget that you are not alone in this journey and that I, just like your friends and family, am here to help guide you to a better life.

Please join me in the next chapter as we take a closer look at both sides of anxiety and how they impact the different aspects of our daily lives. You'll come to see that anxiety can be good in some situations, and by learning to embrace that good nature, you can overcome some of the worrisome thoughts that are holding you back from living life to the fullest.

CHAPTER 2

ANXIETY: A DOUBLE-EDGED SWORD

Anxiety is often seen as purely bad. Everyone has experienced a little bit of anxiety in their lives, and typically it comes when we least expect it, and especially when we don't want it. This means that it brings unwanted symptoms and side effects, all of the things we've discussed in Chapter One. Typically, because of these diverse symptoms we face both physically and mentally, we see anxiety as a sort of evil presence in our lives. Even though science tells us it is a necessary evil, that doesn't negate the fact that it causes us trouble in all different aspects of our lives. Thankfully, we can take a look at the good side of anxiety to help us better understand why we experience it and how it can help us in certain situations. The more we understand our anxieties and fears, especially the ones we feel we have no control over, the easier it is to find solutions and overcome the worry and panic we too often face.

Anxiety is often seen as this bad presence because of the fear that comes along with it, but it is the very fear that causes our anxiety in the first place that is designed to help us survive. In our modern world, we aren't faced with as many obstacles and challenges as we once were during the course of evolution. Even just a couple of centuries ago, humans were faced with many obstacles that threatened their very survival. Everything from plagues to droughts to invading armies, the human race has been through a lot. Somewhere along the way, nature decided we needed a safety system to help us be ready to go to battle or find safety at a moment's notice. This is the adrenaline we find rushing through our veins when we are faced with a moment of fear or stress.

The first thing we must understand when it comes to the two sides of anxiety is that both are fueled by the same innate response to the stressors and triggers we face every day. Our bodies are simply responding to our thoughts and the worrying we accumulate based on our fears. The longer we allow ourselves to dwell on something, the more that thought can take over and drive the anxiety we are trying so hard to push away. There's a whole process to how an anxiety attack or a moment of panic overwhelms us and takes over our very being, which is something we will go over in depth in the following chapters. For now, let's take a moment to further understand the good and the bad of anxiety so that we can identify our triggers and resolve our problems before they grow into something we cannot control.

STRESS IS A NATURAL AND ACCEPTABLE FLAW

When I began to seek out advice and information about my own anxiety, I was faced with this truth as well. I wanted to get rid of anxiety completely because how on earth could it help me if it made me feel so awful? It took me time to truly understand the benefits of anxiety and for me to know that it's okay not to be the most confident or the strongest person in the room at all times. Feeling a little anxious and nervous in different situations is perfectly normal. We are human, and we all feel things differently than the next person, and that's what makes humankind as a collective so unique.

I think, for myself anyway, that we are often trying to compete with others so that we look our best and behave the way we think society expects us to. All this does is making us suppress our true feelings and emotions, and we end up hiding who we really are. It's important to be yourself, especially around people who love and care about you so that they can help you when you are in need. In my early days with anxiety, I found myself pretending to be someone I wasn't so that I didn't look like a nervous wreck in front of my friends. I tried to be more confident and self-assured, but because it wasn't truly me it only made me feel less like myself. And, while I can't speak for others, when I'm not feeling like myself, my anxiety increases seemingly out of nowhere. If I'm not me, then I instantly start thinking that something is wrong, which partly drives my personal anxiety. It is this realization that I want to share with you as my reader because I believe it is something a lot of people do without realizing it.

As a woman, I believe that the stresses that fall on us as mothers and sisters, as well as caretakers in general, are unique in the world of behaviors and mental illnesses. We are sought after to help others feel better. We are the nurturers, and we bring life into the world. Nothing is more important to us than the people we care for, and that most definitely includes our children.

If we think back to a time when civilization was first settling in, we can analyze how the stresses of motherhood have created a unique anxiety for women everywhere. This isn't to say that men do not feel this as well. But there is something unique about how women from thousands of years ago took on the role of caretaker for their children as well as other children in their tribes, that now lingers until today. Even though we lived very different lives than our ancestors, those behaviors and perceptions are still with us in our modern age.

One thing in particular that I believe fuels a lot of anxiety in women is just how dependent we were on the other women in our tribes thousands of years ago. This example comes from something I once read in a magazine about psychology. During the early times of civilization, there were no other means to feed your baby besides breast milk. Imagine if, for whatever reason there might be, you were unable to feed your baby. Or, just the same, something prevented you from caring for your child in one way or another. Who else would help you see to the survival of your child other than the women of your tribe? It would be up to them to help you ensure that your infant survived until childhood when the chances of them living to adulthood became greater.

Because women needed the support of the other women they lived with throughout their entire lives, it was crucial that they got along and worked together. The men would leave for hunting or other purposes, and women had to do everything they could to help their children. If a young mother were at odds with the rest of the women in the tribe, there would be a very good chance that she would not get help when needed. If she fell ill or was otherwise unable to care for her child, there was no guarantee that the other women would help that child either.

What the psychology reading had taught me was that even though these events happened thousands of years ago, and now in our modern world, we have things such as baby formula and daycare services, we are still very much susceptible to the opinions and judgments of the other women in our communities. We seek out their advice and knowledge, and we look for their guidance in many aspects of our lives, not just with our children. Women have a certain sisterhood, and they use that to continue to survive through many different situations that they face on a daily basis. Even if we believe we have everything put together and we are certain that our children will succeed in everything they attempt to do, we will still feel a bit of that anxiousness in the presence of other mothers and women.

This is a bit of good anxiety but also leads to the bad. While it is important to create a sense of community so you can further your survival and grow every day in your life, we often spend too much time dwelling on this topic, letting those thoughts of fear consume us. We wonder whether we are good enough to be friends with certain women. We wonder if we're doing well enough with our children. When we see other women at places such as grocery stores and schools, we feel as though we are being judged, even if the other women do not mean to make us feel this way. We do because we happen to judge others just the same.

We want to know that our families are in the right environment for success, which is why we overanalyze the people who teach our children, the person who brings us our food at the restaurant, and the nurse at the doctor's office who interacts with our babies. We can't escape this fact, but we can appreciate it and acknowledge it for the help it provides. Making the right choices for our loved ones is hard enough. Adding in anxiety doesn't help things along. Instead, we can catch ourselves before we fall into those worrisome thoughts, and we can rise out of the fear knowing that the other women we see every day are feeling this same thing.

ANXIETY IS A TWO-FACED MONSTER

As you well know, there are two sides to every story, and with anxiety, that includes the good and the bad. As we've discussed, many diverse side effects and symptoms come along with the bad side of anxiety. They can be difficult to handle and sometimes feel like they'll never go away. With proper treatment, as you learn to understand yourself more with each passing day, you can overcome this bad side of anxiety and learn to accept the good side to help keep you motivated in your life and connected to those you love most.

The Negative Side of Anxiety

Anxiety is known for being the weighty presence we all fear. Sweaty palms and jittery legs quickly steal our focus and make us hyperaware of the fear we are feeling. Suddenly, the noises around us are louder, and the lights have become brighter. We feel alone and afraid, and the more we fall into these thoughts, the further we slip from reality.

This is the negative side of anxiety, for sure. We feel helpless to hush the thoughts that are keeping us hindered, and we sit silently in the eyes of others, crying out from the growing darkness within. It's an abyss where no one hears or sees unless we make the first move.

As heartbreaking as this is, it is only the beginning. With an anxiety attack (or a panic attack), as it is recognized by professionals, a wild assortment of symptoms begins to take hold. The fidgetiness and clammy skin mentioned earlier are just two of the many things we experience during an attack. Depending on what we are thinking and the obstacles we are facing, these attacks can include countless feelings and fears and may go on for hours or even days.

Let's take a deeper look at how our bodies and minds react to the anxiety we feel as an attack begins to take hold.

At first, the fear we wish to escape enters our minds, but sometimes we don't even realize it until it's too late. Worry begins to overwhelm us. The dread of what may happen fills us. Our hearts begin to pound, heat rises up through our bodies, and we feel that terrible sense of doom weighing us down.

Fear is, of course, a strange thing. We can experience an entire episode of anxiety simply because of the notion of fear. For example, if we are afraid of spiders, just the idea of a spider can create a frenzy in our nerves, minds, and physical bodies without us ever truly spotting a spider at all. It is our fear of something unwanted that drives the anxiety. Even if the fear is not obvious, we must accept that it is there.

After the doom and panic set in, we lose our focus and become prisoners to our minds. Not only has that fear taken root, but it is now beginning to grow. Here, we find ourselves becoming aware of the anxiety, and the second that happens, we start to feel embarrassed and uncomfortable. We know what happens next and, at times, it scares us even more than the fear that has caused the anxiety in the first place.

Imagine for a moment you're having a ladies' night party with your friends. Perhaps you've been dreading this night because of the constant and expected social interaction coming with parties, but you've also been excited. Seeing your friends for an exciting girls' night is supposed to be a blast, but the idea of interacting with so many different people has your nerves in a mess.

We've all been here before. You're thinking about canceling to avoid the situation entirely, but you want to go. Even though dwelling over what might happen at the party has given you a terrible case of insomnia, you just can't pass on a chance to see the girls. You are, however, feeling nervous and anxious. And it's because you're afraid they may judge and ridicule you for whatever small reason you can conjure.

These thoughts are irrational and rooted in fantasy, but we believe them as truths. And before long, our bodies do too. Our muscles tighten and begin to spasm. We can no longer control our fine movements without jerking around like we've had too much caffeine! This may very well happen while talking about the event to a loved one or during the day when we're getting ready. But if it occurs during the party itself, then a full-blown panic attack is sure to ensue.

- Tight muscles and soreness from tension.
- Aching joints from head to toe.
- Nausea and other digestive stresses.
- Trembling hands and overall clumsiness.
- Difficulty focusing and paying attention.

After these feelings and symptoms set in, we begin the process of regret. We wish badly we hadn't acted as we did. We see ourselves negatively and begin to feel ashamed of the nervousness and flighty responses that anxiety has forced upon us. Sometimes during the panic attack, and almost always afterward, we let our minds take hold of us one more time as we assess everything that has happened. This is where we are often too hard on ourselves as we start to regret and wish things had gone differently. This can easily lead to self-doubt and depression, and it can cause us to feel embarrassed, shameful, and upset. It can also push us to seek out ways to remove these feelings, ways that might involve drugs and alcohol as an escape from reality. The biggest problem with this is that we are already escaping from reality by letting ourselves succumb to our thoughts. We must ground ourselves in the present moment because it is our thoughts and our fears that are driving the anxiety to take over our lives.

Before the cycle can begin again, we may find ourselves having trouble sleeping, and we may also feel a general sense of malaise as we think about the next time the situation will arise. For example, if these panic attack symptoms occur during your weekly shopping trip, then each day that comes closer to the next week's trip will provide more anxiety and fear. What's worse is how we begin to overanalyze our panic attacks and start feeling as though they are inevitable in that particular situation in which they first arrived. Before long, we start to fear the fear, and that is when our symptoms become almost inescapable unless we confront them head-on and begin working to move past them.

Given the opportunity, our fears and anxiety can easily take hold and push us further away from reality. This can create fatigue and a lack of concentration, and it can easily wear down your confidence in all aspects of your life. This is why anxiety can be detrimental to everything from your job to your relationships to a simple doctor's appointment, no matter how necessary. Seeking help to identify your triggers and learn ways of keeping yourself grounded in your present surroundings is the only way to reduce these symptoms and take your life back.

The Positive Side of Anxiety

Even though we'd like to equate anxiety to all the negative things coming along with it, we must also understand that good things come from anxiety as well. Humanity might not have survived its early days if it wasn't for our minds recognizing stresses and dangers and our bodies being capable of doing what was necessary to escape or defend. While this is all good, it doesn't help us as much in the modern world. But if we take a moment to look at the different things anxiety can do to help us in our contemporary daily lives, then we can see just how beneficial anxiety can truly be.

Just like throughout human history, we are still faced with moments of danger. Sometimes we have to go beyond our normal capabilities to prevent a catastrophe or escape a situation that otherwise threatens our survival. These types of occurrences include car accidents, natural disasters, and situations involving other people or animals that could harm us. When we need to be stronger than we normally are, think with more focus, and react faster than ever, we rely on the symptoms coming with anxiety to help us attain this.

Because anxiety can give us that rush of adrenaline to get us ready to do the things we would normally do with our physical strength and the way we process the stuff within our environment, it can actually help us sharpen our awareness and react quickly to the dangers around us. I know what you must be thinking. Didn't I just make the point that anxiety as a symptom will sometimes cause a lack of focus and confusion? Yes, indeed, I did. But that kind of anxiety is slightly different from the anxiety we get when faced with a true life-or-death situation. As opposed to the anxiety we have created simply because of our fearful thoughts, the anxiety that helps us escape situations that threaten our livelihood is the real and truest form of anxiety that our bodies and minds have sharpened all throughout evolution.

Instead of standing in line at the grocery store and feeling nervous about the thoughts of others, thinking they might be judging you or criticizing every move you make, this good form of anxiety is specifically designed to ensure that we survive. For example, when our bodies produce adrenaline to escape a house that has caught on fire, we don't sit there and dwell on the possibilities of what might happen. We get up, kick into action, and save the people we love as well as ourselves from the danger.

Anxiety also has other good purposes that don't always involve life-or-death situations. It can help us become more aware of our surroundings so that we can be more empathetic to the people we interact with. The heightened sense of awareness that we get from anxiety can help us to connect with our present reality so long as we learn to recognize it and use it to our benefit rather than allow our thoughts to take over in a fearful state of mind. Being nervous in a situation when you are meeting new people, for example, simply means that you are more intuitive and willing to consider other people and their thoughts and feelings along with your own. The environment will feel more vibrant in this state of mind, and you'll be able to pick up on things you may not have seen before. Yes, this might create a flurry of uncertainty as you weigh the idea that others are forming opinions of you, but do not fret! You are open and vulnerable to a new experience, which shows bravery and courage to your new potential friends!

This is just another way to look at the good side of anxiety, as it shows you that you are a kind and caring person who is truly conscious about the world around them. Don't let doubt cloud this wonderful experience because being a good person like this will surely help you to create beautiful relationships throughout your life.

What we have to be careful of is when we allow our minds to fall deeper into the fear instead of taking hold of the good and the rewarding possibilities coming with anxiety. Delight in the wonder of the moment as you pull yourself out of those pesky, worrisome thoughts. Use the nervousness to your advantage by letting your boldness shine through. It can help you build stronger relationships as you become more accepting of yourself and, therefore, others who you care most about. Just imagine how incredible it will feel to leave behind the shy and lonely you for an empowered version of your best self!

NEGATIVE EFFECTS ON RELATIONSHIPS

Relationships are perhaps one of the first things to suffer when it comes to anxiety. This is because, as the social creatures we are, we are incredibly aware of how other people perceive us in our daily activities. We know that others analyze us and make assumptions based on our behaviors and the way we present ourselves in any given situation. The thought of this alone can drive heavy amounts of anxiety for many people, which is why social anxiety is one of the most prevalent forms of anxiety.

Coping with social anxiety can help to better your relationships with all different types of people, whether you know them very well or they are your childhood friend. We can get anxiety from speaking to someone at a restaurant, even if that someone will only be in our life for a mere hour. We can also get anxiety from speaking to our significant others, which can create a lot of tension and enhanced fear as this is the person you see day after day.

Anxiety in a personal relationship can create unwanted behaviors such as extreme dependency or isolation. When a person is fearful of being left alone and cannot stand the thought of their significant other walking away from the relationship, that person may become increasingly dependent and clingy. On the other hand, when a person is fearful of being judged or analyzed by their significant other, they may begin to isolate themselves to avoid the situation entirely.

These can also apply to other types of relationships, such as close friends, mothers and daughters, brothers, etc. The activities and events that may have once brought you joy could cause great panic over time if you don't see the symptoms for what they are. Before long, you sink deeper and deeper into your thoughts and allow them to take hold over your reality. The things you are fearful of may seem to be inevitable, such as being left by your loved ones and having to continue on alone. In reality, however, there are no reasons to back your assumptions except for an irrational fear that has been allowed to wreak havoc on your thoughts.

In a romantic relationship, it is possible also to suffer a loss of libido as you withdraw further into your mind and away from the present situation. Perhaps your anxiety is rooted in the fear that you are not beautiful enough or good enough for your partner, and thus you avoid situations of intimacy. The more isolated you are from your partner, the less likely it is that you will become intimate, further increasing the loss of libido as you put a wedge between you and the person you love.

At this point, it's important to understand that the people in your life who are there for you time and again do not judge you for little nuances, and most definitely not because you are not beautiful enough. It can sometimes be hard to realize this as our world is filled with vanity. But embracing your anxiety and allowing others to see you for who you truly are will help you see them for who they are as well. Your real friends and family who truly care about you will not be pushed away because of your anxiety. Instead, they will want to help because they truly care and wish the best for you.

Let's take a look at a personal story of a woman who struggled with anxiety in her relationship with her husband. Overcoming her anxiety took time, but once she understood herself and accepted her anxiety as part of her, she could face her relationship head-on and be true to who she was and what she needed out of life.

A Personal Story

Nadia and her husband Adam have been married for several years. After being college sweethearts, they began their life in New York City, focused on their careers like so many others. Nadia works in technology, meaning she spends a good portion of her day sitting at a desk. As she and her husband focused on working long hours to create savings for their dream future, she put little focus on her health. Late-night takeouts and hours behind the desk caused her to gain twenty pounds in her first year of work. As she was already feeling the need to lose ten pounds at the end of college, this made her feel less beautiful as time went on.

As work ramped up and the opportunity for additional hours and pay increased, Nadia could not help but take the opportunity. Near the end of the second year at her new job, Nadia found she had gained another fifteen pounds. Even though she swore she would take up an exercise class and watch her diet, her work consumed her, and she had little time to focus on herself. Because of her busy schedule, which would sometimes conflict with Adam's, Nadia realized she was less and less intimate with her husband.

This is where her fears began to turn into anxiety. She believed her husband wasn't interested in her anymore as she didn't look the same way she did when they first fell in love. They rarely had time for one another, and she started to see it as if he was avoiding her rather than simply being busy with his own work. A little more time went by, and Nadia and Adam interacted less and less. Nadia was certain her husband was growing tired of her and would eventually ask for a divorce. After all, they did not have children yet, and they both had well-paying jobs where they could live a decent life on their own. Nadia felt as though there was nothing truly tying her and Adam together.

One night, after the couple had a big fight, Nadia pointed out how Adam wasn't interested in her anymore. He thought it was ridiculous. He knew that their jobs had consumed them to the point of exhaustion. Because each of them truly loved one another, they were able to discuss their feelings and get to the root of the true problem that was causing Nadia's anxiety. Adam, seeing how the fear of losing the person she loved conflicted Nadia so deeply, made it a point to clear away any doubt his wife had. Adam brought Nadia back into the present reality, grounding her in what was truly going on around them as he pulled her out of her fearful thoughts. And he did this simply by pointing out one thing she had not noticed over the past two years. Adam himself had also gained extra weight and had begun to feel as though Nadia was no longer interested.

With this realization, both Nadia and Adam were able to laugh about their anxiety for a moment before getting to the real work. They both felt as though their youth and beauty were slipping away, and the time that they spent together was narrowing with each passing year. Even though the careers they had chosen were doing them well financially, they had to be honest about what it was doing to them mentally and physically. They were not sleeping well or eating properly as their schedules demanded every bit out of them that they could offer. Nadia and Adam realized it was time for a change.

Nadia sought out a new position with a different company, one where she could have more time at home to prepare healthy meals and take walks in the evenings. Adam did the same. The following year, they felt healthier and happier than they expected, both dropping twenty pounds and feeling like they had more energy to do the things that brought them joy. Nadia and Adam grew close once again, and their true love shined even brighter as they had gone through something difficult and emerged together, stronger because of it.

No longer does Nadia feel as though she isn't beautiful enough for Adam because she realized she never saw him any differently when he had gained weight compared to their college years. She always loved him and wanted to be with him intimately, which showed her that he felt the same. By being realistic about her fears and speaking to the person she loved most about why she was feeling anxious, Nadia was able to resolve her doubts with an actionable plan that has given her a better quality of life in so many ways.

This is just another example of how important it is to reflect upon ourselves and see where we are in our lives and what we want out of them. If we cannot be honest with ourselves, and if we cannot face the things that are troubling us most, we can never expect to heal and grow. Sometimes, it'll take a lot of work to get ourselves out of a situation that is causing us stress and fear. Other times, it might be as simple as taking a walk to clear our minds and get a little much-needed exercise.

WHAT HAVE WE LEARNED?

In this chapter, we've discussed the different sides of anxiety, as well as how anxiety impacts our relationships.

- Stress is necessary as it helps us resolve and avoid dangerous situations.
- Bad forms of anxiety occur when our thoughts run away, and we are unable to come back to the present.
- Good forms of anxiety can push us to become better people, to be more compassionate, and to reach our goals in both our personal and professional lives.
- Anxiety can drive a wedge between two people, but by being honest and open, we can connect with others in a way that builds beautiful and meaningful relationships.

MOVING AHEAD

Now that we can see the importance of both the good and the bad side of anxiety and how letting others see us for who we truly are can help us heal and move forward, we can take a deeper look at each type of anxiety. In the following chapter, we will go through the various forms of anxiety, and in the chapter after that, we will address exactly how to deal with each one of them.

Some of these types of anxiety may resonate clearly with you, and you might also find that a couple of them go hand in hand. Again, do not be hard on yourself if you start to realize you are suffering from different forms of anxiety. This is an important step on the road to recovery and a milestone moment in understanding who you truly are.

So, please join me in the next chapter as we dive deeper into these different types of anxiety that many people across the globe face day after day. Remember that you are not alone in this struggle. I, and so many others, have felt what you are feeling, and I want to help you overcome the stress and emotional weight that anxiety has brought into your life. Allow me to continue to help as we look at the different types of anxiety and what you can do to help alleviate them as soon as today.

CHAPTER 3 PART A

PART A: THE DIFFERENT TYPES OF ANXIETY

...

Dealing with anxiety is difficult enough on its own but trying to understand exactly what type of anxiety you have so that you can find better solutions for your lifestyle can become a monumental stress. As we've discussed, it's important to dig deep and make sense of the anxiety you're facing so that you can truly understand the fears that are holding you back. Sometimes our greatest fears come from not understanding what is happening to us. It is then that we start to make up ideas, and then our thoughts run away from us. This, unfortunately, is exactly what anxiety is made of.

As we go through this chapter, I want you to keep in mind how important it is to listen to yourself first and then try to make sense of the different definitions as they apply to you. You don't want to see a certain type of anxiety listed here and then begin to believe that it is the one affecting you without digging all the way down to know for sure you were right. Sometimes these anxieties will overlap with each other, and that can cause additional symptoms and stress that you may not initially expect. A misdiagnosis of a mental illness can lead to the wrong treatments and only prolong your suffering. Remember that being true to yourself right here is the only way to start alleviating your symptoms and anxiety.

On that note, it's no surprise that with so many different types of personalities and perceptions across the globe, we are faced with a plethora of anxieties. For any type of fear or phobia, there are studies and explanations from medical journals as well as personal stories to give us clarity and hope. To begin this chapter, I think it's best to review some of the anxiety stories that involve some of the celebrities we all know so well. These people are the types who look as though they don't get anxiety, and thus they are the ones we strive to be like. But the truth is, as we've discussed already, everybody experiences it occasionally.

THE CELEBRITIES AND ATHLETES WHO BATTLE ANXIETY JUST LIKE YOU

Sometimes we look to celebrities to better understand ourselves and to reach out to someone we feel we know well enough to model ourselves after. This can sometimes hurt us when we idolize people for their beauty or status, especially when living up to those standards is almost impossible. But comparing ourselves when it comes to the things that make us human and seeking advice and guidance from the faces we love to see week after week on media can often help us move past the things that are keeping us down.

For example, actress Emma Stone has suffered from panic attacks that began when she was only eight. In an interview with The Coaching Room, she recalled visiting a friend and believing the house was on fire. From there, she would ask her mother to tell her how the day would go, constantly checking to be sure everything was set and orderly. She wanted to be sure that no one was going to get hurt or die and that things wouldn't change. Time helped her most in overcoming this anxiety, but also speaking to others and fully understanding how she felt made a big impact.

Superstar Ariana Grande has dealt with anxiety her entire life. After going on tour, she told Seventeen Magazine that she had experienced the most severe anxiety she had ever known. She also remarked about the Manchester Arena bombing from 2017 that occurred during her concert. The event has given her PTSD. She has explained that time helps, but because she is such an advocate for mental health awareness, she also takes the time to speak out for others. Sharing one's story is a form of therapy, and in doing so, we can help each other as we help ourselves.

For actress Lili Reinhart, therapy and medication were lifesavers. Her struggles with depression were triggered by school and have lasted over a decade. She still has days where she feels "really deflated," and on those days, she reminds herself that there is always tomorrow. Depression has also struck Selena Gomez, and it made her realize she needed help. After getting her diagnosis, she felt both "terrified and relieved." This pushed her to launch Mental Health 101, a way to help educate people about their mental health. She explained, "If I had learned about my mental health earlier on—been taught about my condition in school the way I was taught about other subjects—my journey could have looked very different."

Miley Cyrus is an outspoken proponent of mental health aware-ness, and she routinely lives her life openly and allows her fans to know her on a personal level. After the pandemic, Cyrus was clear with her audience that being isolated for so long had taken its toll and that being back on stage brought her closer to panic. This was strange for her since she'd always felt at ease performing. She has worked on researching the mental health and addiction of her family's past, which has helped her better understand how her own mind works.

Supermodel Bella Hadid is candid about her struggles with anxiety and loneliness. She frequently posts crying selfies on social media to show people how human she is. Things as simple as getting ready in the morning gave her anxiety. The use of pictures also helped her explain her feelings to her mother and doctor when she felt unable to express herself. That allowed her to connect with the people who could help her in ways she might not have otherwise.

Anxiety affects many types of people, and that includes singers, actors, and sports stars. David Beckham, for example, has discussed his own struggles with obsessive-compulsive disorder, which have caused him to become very anxious when he doesn't have things perfectly in order. To overcome this desire, Beckham regularly plays Legos with his children, which allows him to control the chaos. Singers Adele and LeAnn Rimes are both familiar with anxiety as well. Even though these women have experienced incredible success, they both have gone through debilitating panic attacks and anxiety that have even pushed LeAnn Rimes into rehabilitation.

Perhaps one of the most iconic and recognizable stars in Hollywood, Johnny Depp has publicly admitted that he battles with panic and anxiety on a daily basis. It has gotten bad enough to where he asks his therapist to travel with him and to be around while he is filming so that he can get through his day with a positive mindset.

Dealing with trauma but always keeping her head up and her mind focused on bettering her life and the lives of other women around her, Oprah Winfrey has dealt with anxiety throughout most of her life. Her fears and panic have come from a form of PTSD from childhood abuse, as well as the losses she experienced throughout her life.

These stories, as well as countless others, just go to show that no matter what you do in life, no matter how successful you may become, or how beloved you are, anxiety is still a part of our human nature. It is something we must learn to accept and heal from the inside out, or it will continue to get the best of us and control us at every turn.

THE SIX MAIN TYPES OF ANXIETY

There are various types of anxiety that affect all different types of people. This is why it's so important to understand that you're not alone in your fight against this mental illness. Even if it seems like you're struggling against something you are positive no one else can understand, the fact is that they also might be struggling against something they believe you couldn't understand. With anxiety, the truth is that we are highly empathic people, and we feel things so heavily that it would be almost impossible for us not to understand someone else's struggles.

Because no two people will live the same life, anxiety can affect us in many different ways. This goes back to the reasons for anxiety, such as environmental factors and physiological composition, and it continues to reinforce the idea that no two people are alike. Even if there are twins who experience anxiety, chances are that anxiety may be felt and perceived differently from one twin to the next simply because of physiology and brain chemistry. The same can be said for families, entire cultures, and the millions of people who fall in between.

Here we will take a look at the different types of anxieties you may or may not have experienced yourself. Sometimes these anxieties can overlap, and other times, they can be so specific that the root of it revolves around a particular memory or trauma. Let's take a minute to examine these common types of anxieties from an outside perspective to gain a deeper understanding of what each one represents so that we can move on to the next chapter and look at how they can be treated. Remember that our ultimate goal is for you to live a happy and healthy life without the fear and doubt imposed by anxiety. The only way to achieve that goal is to fully understand the fears you are up against so you are ready to battle them in the most effective way.

Generalized Anxiety Disorder

For people with generalized anxiety disorder, worrying about certain things throughout their daily lives becomes overbearing. They may experience fear and stress on more days throughout the week than they would not. Generalized anxiety disorder is considered generalized simply because it can involve many different types of anxiety and fear, and different types of stressors can trigger it. Certain things that seem worrisome for people without anxiety disorders will be heightened in people who face generalized anxiety disorder. GAD is diagnosed when a person finds it difficult to control worry on more days than not for at least six months and has three or more symptoms. This differentiates GAD from worries that may be specific to a set stressor or for a more limited period of time.

- GAD affects 6.8 million adults or 3.1% of the U.S. population, yet only 43.2% receive treatment.
- Women are twice as likely to be affected as men. GAD often co-occurs with major depression.

Carson Daly and His Life-Long Battle with General Anxiety Disorder

GET A GRIP! ANXIETY | 53

As a famous television show host, Carson Daly has racked up quite an impressive career. Hosting from the infamously popular *Total Request Live* on MTV to the *Today Show* to *The Voice*, Daly has had plenty of prolific moments. But even the most composed and calmest can have bouts with mental struggles.

"Things are not what they seem, and people need to know that's okay," Daly tells *USA Today* how he's suffered from panic attacks and heavy anxiety, all of which began after losing his father as a boy. During his live shows, he's explained how he keeps his hand in his pocket to hold on to himself as he waits for the panic to fade.

He goes on to say that simply by trying to understand GAD and talking about it with others has helped him to feel better about his life. While there is still a lot to do in the field of anxiety, Daly is happy to be in a position to showcase real people and their struggles to continue to destigmatize general anxiety disorder as a whole.

Daly adds, "It's just inspiring. I've never had an issue with clinical depression . . ." but when doing *Mind Matters*, the segment he is personally involved in on *The Today Show*, "I have a chance to talk to people who struggle differently than I do with suicidal ideation or depression, and I'm in such awe of the bravery of people."

Sometimes, simply speaking to people can help lift some of the weight we feel with anxiety. The more we identify with others, the less we feel our anxieties and believe our fears. It's all about belonging.

Phobias

With a phobia, people are fearful of specific situations, places, objects, or people. A phobia is rooted in the fear of something generally seen as safe rather than dangerous, as the person will interpret it. Some phobias may not make sense to people who have not experienced the fear, but for those who have, it is almost impossible to stop the worry and stress that come with them.

- Specific phobias affect 19 million adults or 8.7% of the U.S. population.
- Women are twice as likely to be affected as men.
- Symptoms typically begin in childhood; the average age of onset is 7 years old.

Of the many phobias known, these are the most common ones:

- Acrophobia, which is the fear of heights.
- Aerophobia, which is a fear of flying.
- Agoraphobia, which is the fear of being unable to escape a situation.
- Aquaphobia, which is the fear of water.
- Arachnophobia, which is the fear of spiders.
- Blood, injury, and injection (BII) phobia: Fear of injuries involving blood.
- Claustrophobia, which is the fear of being in a small or confined area.
- Dentophobia, which is the fear of dentists.
- Driving phobia, which is the fear of driving a car.
- Emetophobia, which is the fear of vomiting.
- Escalaphobia, which is the fear of escalators.
- Illness anxiety disorder, formally called hypochondria, is the fear of becoming ill or having a serious medical

condition.

- Phobia surrounding blood and injections, which is typically the fear of needles and blood injury.
- Zoophobia, which is the fear of animals.

Diva Madonna and Her Intense Fear of Thunder and Lightning

While Madonna happens to be a powerhouse celebrity, full of confidence and strength, she deals with phobias like many other people across the globe. Known as brontophobia, this fear can cause extreme anxiety, even by just the mention of a storm. People who suffer from this phobia are likely to hide during a storm, even if the thunder is brief and poses no real threat.

Madonna is known to check weather reports religiously before performances. If a storm is approaching, she may cancel. It isn't easy to overcome a fear like this, especially since it cannot be handled in a controlled environment. This is one reason for it being so anxiety-inducing. The mere fact that the thunder is out of her control only causes more fear for Madonna.

Social Anxiety Disorder

When it comes to social anxiety, people experience unending fear of being ridiculed, judged, or evaluated in various negative ways. They feel as though they might get rejected in any given situation that involves interacting with other people. Because of this, people who experience social anxiety disorder will tend to avoid places where they may experience their symptoms and isolate themselves from social environments altogether.

- SAD affects 15 million adults or 6.8% of the U.S. population.

- SAD is equally common among men and women and typically begins around age 13.
- According to a 2007 ADAA survey, 36% of people with social anxiety disorder report experiencing symptoms for ten or more years before seeking help.

How Creating Personal Space Has Helped Kendall Jenner with Her Social Anxiety

As a megastar, Kendall Jenner is familiar with the spotlight. This doesn't mean she is any more okay with it than others. For some, social anxiety can be a living nightmare. Seeing so many people and wondering how they're judging you with each move you make is nothing short of complete terror. With social anxiety, it is all about the interactions, both expected and unexpected, that we deal with every day.

In an Instagram post, Jenner has said, "My anxiety (especially social anxiety) has been on 100 lately. I've come to a place where I don't feel bad about it."

Jenner has let her fans know that she combats her anxiety by creating a personal space for herself where she can be alone. In addition, she begins her days with a positive mindset and with plenty of activities that create a balanced and wholesome mental state. She spends time outside and away from her devices, journals about what she is grateful for, and makes a list of the things she is looking forward to. These practices, along with finding a way to ground oneself and connect with our energies, are sure to help anyone with social anxiety.

Post-Traumatic Stress Disorder

Post-traumatic stress disorder is a mental illness that causes people to revisit traumatic experiences that happened in their past. These can include terrible accidents, war and other violence, natural disasters, and sexual assault. Also known as PTSD, this disorder can become debilitating for people who are unable to process the fear and the weight of the past traumatic experience in order to move forward. They may feel fearful of an immediate disaster, one that forces them to relive their past traumas. They will also experience the symptoms of general anxiety and panic, such as rapid heartbeats, sweating, nervousness, restlessness, and nausea. No matter the type of trauma, each person needs their own time to go through the events that have occurred to them and to understand how it is impacting them in all aspects of their current life.

- PTSD affects 7.7 million adults or 3.5% of the U.S. population.
- Women are more likely to be affected than men.
- Rape is the most likely trigger of PTSD: 65% of men and 45.9% of women who are raped will develop the disorder.
- Childhood sexual abuse is a strong predictor of the lifetime likelihood of developing PTSD.

Actress Gabrielle Union Battles PTSD Every Day of Her Life

Gabrielle Union is a shining light for women everywhere. Her grounded personality is a beacon and also a reminder that she is very human like the rest of us. As a survivor of rape, she spoke with *People Magazine* to bring awareness to mental health.

"As a rape survivor, I have battled PTSD for thirty years. Living with anxiety and panic attacks all these years has never been easy.

There are times when the anxiety is so bad that it shrinks my life. Leaving the house or making a left-hand turn at an uncontrolled light can fill me with terror."

Union continued to explain her struggles, "When we tell y'all what we are experiencing, please believe us the first time we mention it. No, it's not like being nervous and everyone experiences and deals with anxiety differently, and that's okay. I don't need you to try to 'fix' me."

While her anxiety sometimes gets the best of her, she never lets it win. She focuses on reaching out to others to let them know they aren't alone. Building this network of people who can be open about their struggles can help people to rise above and continue to push forward in their lives.

Obsessive-Compulsive Disorder

The symptoms involved with OCD include an obsessive need to behave in compulsory ways, the likes of which sufferers cannot avoid. These can be seen as antics and nuances that a person must complete, such as tapping a doorknob a specific number of times before being able to turn the handle. The behaviors associated with OCD stem from thoughts and anxiety that force the sufferer to believe they must complete the actions in order to avoid unwanted consequences. Some people, for example, may believe that if they do not perform their compulsory behaviors, something terrible will happen to them or the people they love. It is also important to note that not every behavior is visible, and some can be mental and easily hidden.

- OCD affects 2.2 million adults or 1.0% of the U.S. population.
- OCD is equally common among men and women.

- The average age of onset is 19, with 25% of cases occurring by age 14. One-third of affected adults first experienced symptoms in childhood.

Soccer Star David Beckham Uses Legos to Ease His OCD Mind

Notoriously famous superstar David Beckham has long enjoyed building Lego sets with his children. As a person who has spoken about his OCD from time to time, Beckham makes use of the toys to help him relax. "The last big thing I made was the Tower Bridge. It was amazing. I think Legos sometimes help to calm me down," Beckham told *The Sunday Times* back in 2014.

Psychologist Jon Sutton weighed in by saying, "I can see it being very therapeutic for someone with David's personality." As Sutton explained to *The Sunday Times*, "Legos are about making order out of chaos. You get the set out of the box, empty it onto the floor, and start with this mess that you then have to carefully build piece by piece."

Making order from chaos is indeed a great way to focus the efforts of an OCD person into something good and rewarding. This way the anxiety associated with needing to find patterns and perfection will end in a satisfying result.

Panic Disorder

Panic disorder is the tendency to experience panic attacks that seem to start from no visible trigger. The symptoms involved include sweating, rapid heartbeat, worrisome and uncontrollable thoughts, and the fear of impending doom, to name a few. People who suffer from panic disorder will have spontaneous bursts of panic, and sometimes it can be attributed to the fear of having another panic attack itself. It becomes a vicious cycle where a person learns to fear the very fear that their own minds have created. This disorder can affect people of all ages, but it is normally seen in early adulthood. It is also worth noting that women are affected by panic disorder nearly twice as often as men.

- PD affects 6 million adults or 2.7% of the U.S. population.
- Women are twice as likely to be affected as men.

Singer Adele Battles Anxiety by Working Out

During her divorce, Adele experienced horrific panic attacks. Telling Oprah during her *One Night Only* special, Adele said, "I had the most terrifying anxiety attacks after I left my marriage. They paralyzed me completely and made me so confused because I wouldn't be able to have any control over my body. But I was aware of that happening because it was kind of still very much there while my whole body was just, like, on another planet, it felt like."

Because of her debilitating anxiety and panic, she knew she had to get her mind on the right track. In doing so, she found that she enjoyed going to the gym and working out to relieve her stress. This helped her mind to stay clear and focused on something that wasn't giving her anxiety. Over time, it not only helped her overcome those fears, but she also felt better from the healthy change to her lifestyle.

WHAT HAVE WE LEARNED?

This chapter has been a comprehensive review of the various types of anxieties. Throughout, we have discussed:

- The different phobias people may have, including dental phobia, blood and injection phobias, and agoraphobia.
- Obsessive Compulsive Disorder and the need to find order in chaos.
- General Anxiety Disorder and how it differentiates from normal worry.
- The symptoms associated with these different anxieties, and what to look for in both your physical and mental health.
- Several celebrities who struggle with different forms of anxiety and stress and how they combat their symptoms.

The Six Types in Review

- Generalized Anxiety Disorder: Overly excessive worry with no or multiple triggers.
- Phobias: Irrational fear of everyday items or situations.
- Social Anxiety Disorder: Anxiety in social gatherings.
- Post-Traumatic Stress Disorder: Past struggles that resurface.
- Obsessive Compulsive Disorder: The need to find order out of chaos.
- Panic Disorder: Intense fear along with physical symptoms.

MOVING AHEAD

Now that we have a better understanding of the different forms of anxiety, we can move on to the next chapter to look at how we can treat them and make them less of an issue in our daily lives. Never forget as we continue on through this book that there are so many people in your life who experience anxiety just like you, and even the most successful and happy people feel fear and panic. It can be debilitating and can ruin an otherwise perfect day, but with the help of your friends and family and the guidance of this book, you can find real solutions to this dynamic disorder.

As we move on to the next chapter, I'd like you to remember the differences we spoke about here and how they can impact the things we do every day. Finding a way to recover from our fears and progress into a more positive lifestyle takes patience and dedication, but we also have to be observant. We all have our own limitations, and there are countless ways that anxiety can be triggered. And being honest with ourselves and aware of these things will help us to get to the life we wish to have.

CHAPTER 3 PART B

... AND HOW TO DEAL WITH THEM!

Resolving your anxiety and improving your life takes dedication and time. It cannot happen overnight and cannot last unless you take the time to truly understand yourself and how you handle stress. Knowing which type of anxiety you have is half the battle. Now the real work can begin.

PERSONAL STORIES OF CONQUERING EACH TYPE OF ANXIETY

Generalized Anxiety Disorder

Layla was a worrisome child. She would think about the worst that could happen in both real and imaginative circumstances. It took her until her early thirties to see a therapist, and that person was able to finally give Layla the answers she needed. She was suffering from Generalized Anxiety Disorder, and simply knowing what was causing her troubles made things all the more easier.

Phobias

Phobias can present at any age and in any number of combinations. For Alisha, this means dealing with seven of the nine main phobias. Her struggles began with agoraphobia in her early twenties. It started while she was out in public with friends. Any place that felt small and closed off became a threat. Before long, she realized she was having terrible panic attacks, complete with vertigo, rapid heartbeats, and nausea. She explains that the onset of the phobia, to the point where she sought help from being housebound, took only weeks to improve. Her overall recovery, however, would take much longer, even years. She finds that quality rest and time to enjoy her favorite hobbies help her to stay comfortable in her environment.

Social Anxiety Disorder

Ever since her school days, Dana has been plagued by social anxiety. It didn't matter the situation, or whether she had a few or many people around her, she felt the strains and stresses of the intense fears piling high. According to CNN Health, "About 4% of the world population will have social anxiety disorder at some point in their lives, which is roughly 300 million people." For people like Dana, the best option is typically cognitive behavioral therapy, a process that retrains the brain to associate certain feelings with each trigger. This can create more positive reactions to the things that were often negative.

Post-Traumatic Stress Disorder

Trauma can feel different for each person, and depending on their triggers, it can resurface at any moment. For Aliza, dealing with her PTSD, which developed after being assaulted as a student, has meant finding herself in the midst of a chaotic world. Learning about the things she enjoys most, such as the smell of her favorite lotion, coloring, or simply sitting on the floor to feel something other than complete doom, has helped her to remain in the present and clear away her thoughts.

Obsessive-Compulsive Disorder

Needing to have things just a specific way is one hallmark of OCD, as Maria knows well. As someone who loves reading books, she finds that keeping her shelves perfectly aligned and her home completely organized brings both pleasure and pain. On the one hand, it's tiring to keep things so perfectly ordered; on the other, she feels it must be done or something terrible will happen. Perhaps something will fall and break. Maybe something will get lost. While trying to combat her anxiety, she discovered therapy and medications that have been helpful. Of all, cognitive behavioral therapy, CBT, seems to stand out the most. How a person with OCD sees the world is very different from a person without, and that distinction makes CBT so effective.

Panic Disorder

Panic attacks are truly terrible to experience, as Salma can attest to. As a young woman trying to combat her panic disorder, she has found a method that works best for her and many other people she has spoken to about panic attacks: Exercise and eating right. Getting moving can help free up some of the anxiety we feel simply by using up our energy stores. And if we couple that with quality nutrition, we feel the right type of energy and can stay focused and empowered to be our best selves throughout most of the day. She also attributes journaling as a key solution to her struggles. Writing her thoughts and activities down, along with her feelings and emotions with each, keeps her on top of what is working and what isn't.

COPING TRICKS AND TIPS

When anxiety hits us strongly, we sometimes cannot do anything about it except allow it to pass through. This is especially true for people who have certain types of anxiety that seem to happen with no apparent triggers. The following coping mechanisms can help to reduce your stress and anxiety levels before they have a chance to affect you. Some of these tips can also work during an episode.

Physical Strategies

The physical ways we can combat an anxiety attack or help to reduce our stress to make our anxiety less prevalent include the following:

- Staying physically active with exercise and favorite sports.
- Refraining from drug and alcohol use.
- Implementing stress management and relaxation techniques.
- Prioritizing your sleep for a full night's rest.
- Eating foods that provide the proper nutrients and vitamins for your active body.

Emotional and Behavioral Strategies

Emotional strategies will help you to keep your mind focused and relaxed as you tackle the obstacles of your day. Conquering the emotional aspect of an anxiety attack may include the following:

- Researching and understanding your type of anxiety and how to treat it. There is fear behind the things we do not know. Familiarize yourself to make your anxiety less strange and frightening.
- Pay close attention to your episodes to learn what is triggering you. Then you can avoid those triggers for reduced stress and anxiety.
- Begin journaling to better understand your struggles and strengths. Knowing yourself well will help you to accept and love yourself. You will also spot patterns in your mental health this way.
- Use techniques like cognitive behavioral therapy to reduce your negative thoughts. Keep yourself as positive as you can.

Take a little time each day to socialize with others. You'll start to see the world in a new way as you realize everyone around you deals with anxiety in their own way. You'll also feel more occupied, and because of that, you won't dwell on the things that bring you fear.

With these diverse coping tips, you'll be on your way to reversing your anxiety and gaining control over your stress. What it boils down to is this:

- Stay positive.
- Eat healthy foods.
- Remain active.
- Be patient with yourself and take time to learn who you are.

SPOTLIGHT ON DENTAL ANXIETY

Dental anxiety is a well-known form of anxiety that many people face throughout their lives. Some anxiety at the dentist office is simply medical anxiety, which is a fear that something bad will happen to a person's health. This was once identified as hypochondria but is now formally recognized as illness anxiety disorder. People who deal with this form of anxiety are afraid to visit the dentist because they feel that the dentist will find many problems and essentially tell them that their mouth is unhealthy.

This is incredibly frightening and can cause people to feel like all hope is lost when it comes to their oral health. After all, you cannot live without a mouth, so keeping it healthy is an absolute must.

Other people may go into the dentist office frightened of other things like needles, drills, or even the simple fact that other people have used the same chair, as is the case with a person suffering from mysophobia. With this phobia, germs are the culprit, and the person suffering believes nothing can be clean enough.

Let's take a look at the reasons why visiting a dentist is necessary and what can happen if someone puts off oral care.

The Negative Effects on Oral Health as a Result of Anxiety

Not only does anxiety cause us painful physical symptoms and disorienting mental symptoms, but it can also lead to problems in our oral health. The following are some conditions caused by anxiety:

- Dry mouth.
- Canker sores (aphthous ulcers).

- Burning mouth syndrome.
- Bruxism (grinding or clenching of teeth).
- Lichen planus (lacy white lines, red areas, or mouth ulcers on the cheek, gums, or tongue).
- Temporomandibular joint disorder (also commonly known as TMJ or TMD).

Strategies for Reducing or Eliminating Anxiety during Dental Visits

Even though dental anxiety impacts many people, and for some, anxiety is so bad that they avoid visiting their dentist altogether, there are ways to eliminate or greatly reduce the stress and fear. The following options are key in helping you to overcome the struggle of seeing a dentist regularly, which is preventing you from keeping your mouth healthy.

In a survey done by Dental Products Report, more than 60% of people surveyed admit to having a fear of being at the dentist office. As a dentist, this is something I take very seriously. Helping people to feel and become healthier is my goal, and there is so much at stake when a person has an unhealthy mouth. Without proper dental hygiene, the body is more susceptible to other conditions, like heart disease, cancer, and diabetes.

Use the following techniques to create a positive experience for when you visit your dentist next:

- Find a dentist who caters to people dealing with dental phobias. Some dentists are more prepared than others to help patients who experience anxiety with dentistry. These dentists may have a soothing environment, distraction items, comfortable chairs, and equipment, and they will most likely allow you to bring in things to make the experience more positive.

- Communicate your problems with your dentist so that they are well aware of how you feel. Only by doing this can you expect quality treatment for your teeth and mind.
- Utilize breathing exercises to allow your mind and body to feel calmer. Deep breathing is a great way to focus your mind on what is at hand rather than the rapid thoughts of worry that come with anxiety.
- Meditate and incorporate muscle relaxation techniques. Meditation lets us take control over our thoughts as we settle even the most fearsome ideas. During meditation, our muscles relax and release tension that builds from stress. Meditation can be used before, during, and after a dentist visit to help you remain calm and positive.
- Visualization techniques, such as guided imagery, allow us to harness our imagination to make something good out of what we perceive as bad. For example, if the dentist office is a dull and upsetting place to visit, then you can think of a place that makes you happy and focus on it instead. This "happy place" of yours is something you can use for any anxiety, which is what makes it so wonderful. It can be anywhere you want, so long as you can see it in your mind when you close your eyes. Maybe a beach or a forest, or even your comfy room.
- Distracting ourselves is a fantastic way to quiet the anxiety inside and focus on things that bring us joy. Wearing headphones or playing a game on your phone may help you feel better about being at the dentist. You can also take a fidget toy or some other item to play with and keep you from feeling overwhelmed.
- Bringing a friend along can help make the strange dentist office feel more comfortable and familiar. Your friend knows you well and can help by talking to you about things they know you love. The friend can also hold your

hand or give you words of encouragement to make the event less scary.

- Using hypnosis is a little like cognitive behavioral therapy, except you aren't fully aware and in control of the mental changes. With CBT, a person can work to retrain their brain. With hypnotherapy, however, an outside person influences the patient to feel and think in a certain way that can impact their health positively.

- Analgesia is a pain medication that is obtainable over the counter. It is widely available and can help you feel less pain from your oral problems and, thus, less anxiety and tension. Your dentist may even use nitrous oxide, also called laughing gas, at your appointment to ease the pain and worry about your mouth.

- Anxiety-relieving medication can help to remove the anxious feelings while you visit the dentist. Your dentist might even prescribe the medication themselves, providing you with the right dosage for your level of anxiety.

- Conscious sedation is when we choose to take a sedative that will allow us to stay awake and alert, but we will be very relaxed.

- General anesthesia is what doctors use to put people to sleep for short amounts of time. This type of aid is used to make you unconscious during your treatment, so you will not experience any of the anxiety or negativity you may typically have with dentistry. You may have to visit a specialist to receive this type of care, but after the procedure is over, you'll wake feeling relaxed and properly cared for rather than tense and worried.

Finding Peace with the 3–3–3 Rule

There are times when we aren't able to use these tricks to make us feel better. Some of our triggers are not known to us, and they can sneak up when we least expect them. In these moments, if we can bring ourselves back to the moment and into the present, we can regain control over our thoughts and fears.

- Begin by closing your eyes and naming three things you can hear. Really listen to your surroundings and connect with what is happening around you.
- Next, move three parts of your body so that you can feel what is in your environment. Touch something with your hand, step out of your shoes and feel the ground with your bare feet, move around in your chair or take a seat.
- Last, look around and name three things you can see. Diversify these things by choosing items with different colors and textures. Really force yourself to be creative here.

You can also use the other senses to bring yourself back to the present. What do you smell? What do you taste? Perhaps you're in the middle of eating dinner at a restaurant, and you feel panic setting in. Focus on the food: the flavors, textures, the spices. Talk about what you're tasting with someone you know and hold that conversation so that your fearful thoughts have no chance to surface.

WHAT HAVE WE LEARNED?

In this chapter, we have talked in depth about how to treat your anxiety and settle your nerves with proven techniques. These have included:

- Mental and emotional coping strategies to ease your mind.
- Physical strategies to exert energy positively.
- How to handle the six main types of anxiety, and what works best for each.
- The impact of dental anxiety and how you can overcome the symptoms that are keeping you from quality oral care.
- Enlisting the 3–3–3 rule to bring yourself back to the present and beat that panic attack before it takes hold.

MOVING AHEAD

Even though these tricks can help in many ways, sometimes we have to be honest with ourselves about what we can and cannot accomplish on our own. In these times, it may be best to ask for professional help so that we can live our best lives. There's no reason to feel the pain and fear when we can resolve these struggles and brighten each new day with a healthy and positive outlook.

Join me in the next chapter while we explore seeking out professional help. You'll discover when it is best to speak with your doctor about your symptoms and what you can expect from such a visit. Several types of treatments are available for anxiety, and your doctor knows best how to help you find relief and gain control of your life.

CHAPTER 4

SEEKING PROFESSIONAL HELP

Anxiety is a difficult struggle to manage, and sometimes we need the help of others to get through the uphill climb. Even though anxiety is usually self-diagnosable and can be treated in the comforts of your home with self-care therapies and practices, seeking help is also highly beneficial. According to the Anxiety and Depression Association of America:

- "Anxiety disorders are highly treatable, yet only 36.9% of those suffering receive treatment."
- "People with an anxiety disorder are three to five times more likely to go to the doctor and six times more likely to be hospitalized for psychiatric disorders than those who do not suffer from anxiety disorders."

WHEN TO SEE YOUR DOCTOR

It is important to seek out a doctor's help when you feel you cannot manage your symptoms on your own. A psychiatrist can guide you through recovery to get your life back on track in a positive and effective manner. In addition, seek out professional help if:

- Your worry is interfering with your work and your personal relationships.
- The anxiety and fear you have are upsetting you so much that you cannot control your emotions.
- You are depressed and are using drugs or alcohol to make yourself feel better.
- You believe the anxiety you're feeling could be part of a larger mental or physical health problem.

No matter what you are going through or dealing with in your life, if you ever have suicidal thoughts or behaviors, seek emergency medical care immediately. Remember that the fear you are feeling in this moment will pass and that it is not worth ending your life over. There are people who love and care for you and who want to see you live a happy life with many more positive days to come.

Also, it's worth noting that some forms of anxiety, based on chemistry and physiology, may not resolve on their own. In these instances, you must seek out professional help to find the solutions that will work best in your situation. Your anxiety will also be easier to treat if you ask for help early on.

Professional Intervention through Psychotherapy and Counseling

Psychotherapy and counseling are a means of helping one to change their behaviors by addressing the thoughts and feelings that are causing the unwanted reactions. When they address the way you feel and how your emotions play a role in your overall behaviors, they can target those behaviors you wish to stop.

Cognitive Behavioral Therapy, also called CBT, is one of the most well-known types of psychotherapy. With CBT, we look closely at the fears you have and what your thoughts and feelings are behind those fears. After identifying these main components, we can then begin the work to retrain the brain with breathing exercises, relaxation techniques, and positive self-talk.

One form of CBT that is highly effective is exposure therapy. Here, you are slowly exposed to the thing that is causing you fear and anxiety, and over time, you learn to become comfortable with it. This process, which is done in small increments to ensure no relapse in care, allows a person to feel calmer around the things that would normally cause stress.

Professional Intervention through Medication

Proven medication therapies can also help you make progress in your care. Some of these are needed when our anxiety is so high that we can't yet begin with therapies like CBT. To get our minds settled and ready for things like breathing techniques and good old-fashioned self-care, we must first calm the thoughts and emotions holding us in place.

These medications are some of the most commonly prescribed for anxiety and depression:

- Antidepressants can help to alter the levels of certain neurotransmitters in the brain. This may help to ease the symptoms of anxiety.
- Benzodiazepines are an anti-anxiety group of medications that work quickly and are often used as a short-term treatment.
- Beta-blockers are usually used to treat high blood pressure but can also help relieve some of the physical symptoms of

anxiety.

- Tricyclics are a class of drugs older than antidepressants that provide benefits for most anxiety disorders. They are not as effective for OCD.
- Antipsychotics can be used in low doses to help make other treatments work better.
- Buspirone (BuSpar) is an anti-anxiety drug that is sometimes used to treat chronic anxiety.

These medications are only available from your doctor, which is why it is sometimes necessary to ask for professional help when your self-care isn't doing as much as you would like.

Personal Story

As a secretary, Hannah had always spent a vast amount of time working on her computer. Even though the office work kept her busy, she had plenty of time to browse and visit social media sites. The negative energy she gathered from these places seemed to accumulate, and before long, she was feeling depressed and anxious about constant gloom.

Hannah was already a bit of a worrier, and by filling her life with the opinions and misguided advice of others, she was slipping further from her cheerful self each and every day. In addition, she was growing anxious in the company of others, making her want to stay at her desk and not speak to anyone at all. When a coworker spoke about self-care and CBT, she was intrigued. Perhaps it was just what she needed to pull herself free from the darkness.

Hannah sought the advice of a therapist since she had no idea where to start this journey of retraining her brain. The therapist advised that CBT was the perfect option for her as she had developed social anxiety and generalized anxiety from being irrationally fearful of things happening to her and the people she cared about. With the help of the therapist, Hannah was able to use the techniques enlisted with CBT to remove some of the stress and fear from her life, as well as to learn new tricks to keep her positive and focused on what matters most.

Her advice from her experience was simple: Unplug and reconnect with the things that bring you true joy. To do this, you must know yourself well, and you must be willing to take the time needed to dig deep and uncover your truest self. That's where the real work begins, but that also means it's where you'll find the real treasure.

WHAT HAVE WE LEARNED?

In this chapter, we have discussed how seeking professional help is sometimes a necessary step in recovery. There are things a psychiatrist can do for you that can remove some of the struggles you're feeling with your anxiety.

- It's important to see a doctor when you feel like you cannot control your symptoms.
- You must always seek immediate professional care when you're feeling suicidal.
- Self-care techniques work well for many, but sometimes we need a boost, which can be as simple as speaking to a doctor.
- Psychiatrists can prescribe medication that can help you achieve your results faster.

MOVING AHEAD

Finding help from a psychiatrist is always a good option, but thanks to the information age, we can now get help anytime and anywhere. With technology, there are many ways to connect with others to find help and therapies for the anxiety you're feeling.

Join me in the following chapter as we take a look at how technology can play a helpful role in your resolution of the stresses and anxieties you face daily.

MAKE A DIFFERENCE WITH YOUR REVIEW

Unlock the Power of Generosity

"Every act of kindness creates a ripple with no end."

— UNKNOWN

Imagine if each kind word you said could wrap around someone like a comfy blanket on a chilly night. That's what your review could do for someone out there!

So here's my big favor I'm asking, with a cherry on top.

Would you be an undercover hero for someone you've never met? Someone who might be feeling the same butterflies or stormy thoughts you felt before?

We're all on a mission—a super important one—to share the secrets inside 'Get A Grip! Anxiety' with everyone who's ever nibbled their nails with nerves or felt like their heart was doing jumping jacks.

This is where you, yes YOU, shine like the stars.

Did you know that lots of people decide to read a book based on what people like you say about it? And now, I have a simple mission for you, perfect for a caring person like yourself for all the worriers out there who are wrestling with worries:

Would you help a buddy out by sharing your thoughts on this book?

It's entirely complimentary (truly, not a penny required), and less than 60 seconds to make it real. This modest gesture holds immense value in the eyes of another.

Your heartfelt review can serve as the gentle encouragement that aids...

...someone wrestling with nerves to remember they aren't walking this path alone.
...a fellow seeker gains the strength to say, "I understand, for I too have been there."
...a brother or sister in faith realizes they have a companion on this journey.
...or even help a small but precious hope take root and flourish.

To truly make a positive impact and offer genuine assistance to this individual...

Please rate and leave a review.

- **Enjoyed the book on Audible?** Just click the three dots in the top right, hit 'rate & review', and leave your thoughts with a star rating.
- **Reading on Kindle or another e-reader?** Swipe up at the end, and it'll guide you to leave a review.
- **Can't find these options?** No worries. Head over to the book's page on Amazon or where you bought it and post your review there.

- **Or simply scan the <u>QR Code</u> below with your smartphone to share your insights directly:**

If the thought of helping someone makes your heart warm, you're really shining bright!

Go ahead and pat yourself on the back.

You're part of something really kind and beautiful!

I'm so excited to show you how to say, "No worries!" and face anxiety with strength in our next chapters. Get ready to be hugged by the brave boosts we've got just for you.

Thank you, tons, and tons! Let's flip to the next part of our adventure together.

Cheering you on,

S A Nightingale

P.S. Remember when you share helpful stuff, you're someone's hero.

Think 'Get A Grip! Anxiety' could be a beacon for someone else.

Your kind review could be just the light they need to keep the hope and courage shining bright!

CHAPTER 5

TAPPING THE POWER OF TECHNOLOGY

Technology is like a double-edged sword for people with anxiety. Ever since social media became the main form of connecting with others, we as a global culture have become addicted to seeking out our peers for approval and gratitude. This pleasure-seeking activity that almost all of us engage in is now a part of our routines.

With the anxiety that social media places on our daily lives, it's no wonder people are seeking new methods to combat their mental health in new and innovative ways. After an entire generation has gone through the information age and has felt the strain and constriction that has come along with repeatedly checking social media feeds for that instant gratification, it's no wonder that the new generation is also looking at technology as a way to help fight anxiety and depression.

Not only has technology been mentally invasive and persistent in our modern lives, being in all sorts of places like schools, businesses, and even our homes, but it is also often nerve-racking to our physical health. People have begun developing something known commonly as "tech neck." Also called "Dowager's Hump" in the medical community, it is when a curvature of the thoracic vertebrae occurs, and a visible hump extends outward at the base of the neck. It comes from hunching over, most often when texting, browsing our computers, or even playing video games.

In addition, there are harmful effects of blue light on the eyes, which can cause eye strain and headaches, and there are also the dangers of sitting around too much. This can lead to weight gain, heart problems, diabetes, and muscle weakness.

Technology isn't terrible or in need of removal from our lives, but it is something we must utilize in moderation. And when we use it to help better our lives, such as researching helpful things about diet and exercise and connecting with our mental health professionals, technology can help save lives.

With the future at our fingertips, we are finding new and innovative ways to use technology for the benefit of mental health. The therapies available to us are endless in our current world, and they come in the forms of applications, virtual reality, and artificial intelligence. We are truly on the precipice of connecting humanity to technology in ways never seen before.

VIRTUAL REALITY THERAPY

In the world of gaming, most people are aware of what is known as VR: virtual reality. Just as the name suggests, it is a way to submerge yourself into a reality that is completely virtual. This means you can simulate yourself into a game setting on another planet simply by sitting on your couch and using a headset. Thankfully, mental health professionals have found a way to use it to help patients overcome their fears in a fast and effective adaptation of CBT.

When a person uses virtual reality as a means to implement cognitive behavioral therapy, they wear the headset and submerge themselves into a situation that would typically cause them stress and anxiety. For example, if someone feels social anxiety in a public setting like a grocery market, they can "visit" a market setting in VR in small increments until they feel more comfortable. This is a controlled form of exposure that can greatly benefit a person and help them overcome their fears positively.

CHATBOT THERAPY

Many unfortunate things resulted from the coronavirus pandemic, one of which was the strain placed on people's mental health because of isolation. Fortunately, society as a whole answered this dilemma promptly by creating a plethora of mental health apps so people could work through their traumas and stresses and find relief.

One of the main successes of this wave of new health apps is from the Stanford company called Woebot. Along with the psychologists at Stanford, artificial intelligence experts have created an app that offers an automated response entity that will carry on a conversation. This bot is capable of watching the user's mood for current feelings and changes, and it will also talk to the person about their mental health. Woebot is able to share tools and tips that can help a person find more help if required.

There are many apps like Woebot as people are asking for easier ways to care for their mental health. There are artificial intelligent apps that allow a person to make a virtual "friend" who is not real but a simulation. These apps are private, and the user is able to share things that are bothering them. Sometimes just the act of talking through your struggles can make them seem a bit less overbearing and more manageable.

MENTAL HEALTH APPS

Aside from bots and virtual friends, there are other mental health apps that can guide people to finding the right care, as well as offer the care needed. Thanks to the advancements in technology, as well as the demand for more modern and convenient means to see doctors, there are now virtual care visits available to patients from the very comfort of their homes. Speaking with a professional therapist is possible most days and hours of the week, and they are often covered by medical insurance companies just the same. Even when not, virtual visits are sometimes considerably less costly to attend, which makes caring for oneself much easier.

If you happen to be looking for a way to implement a better self-care routine, there are apps for that too. Things like mindfulness practices, journaling, daily gratitude and inspiration, meditation, and mood tracking are highly beneficial in helping someone improve their mental health.

Current Apps That May Help

The following apps are current as of the publication of this book. They are helpful in creating a peaceful and positive environment for you to destress and let go of your fears. Some of them are also great at occupying time without leaving you feeling strung out. Remember, you can also use a blue light filter to help reduce the strain on your eyes while on your phone or laptop.

1. **Calm:** Currently, Calm is one of the most popular and widely used apps for mental health. With it, people can learn to ease their minds through meditation and relaxation techniques, both of which help a person handle stress and anxiety better. In addition, Calm also focuses on

healthy sleep patterns so that the body can recover from the day and start anew.

2. **Headspace:** Because anxiety is everywhere we look, Headspace's targeted meditation aims to lower stress levels by focusing on the specific anxiety a person is experiencing. With topics on aging, politics, body-shaming, and death, Headspace helps its users to learn to find happiness and be kinder to their minds.

3. **Wysa:** This app teaches users stress-coping techniques to improve their mental health. In addition, it also has an AI feature that lets people talk about what they are going through so they can move past what is holding them back. There is a coach option as well for people who wish to speak to a live therapist.

4. **Pacifica:** This app uses some of the same principles in CBT, one of the biggest ones being muscle relaxation. The focus in Pacifica is on generalized anxiety, where users can learn to lessen the tension they feel from fear and stress so they can handle anxiety much better.

5. **Colorfy:** As one of the more creative and game-like apps on the list, Colorfy is a beautifully designed coloring book for adults. Not only does this app help you zone out and relax through focused meditation, but it is also a distraction app that can occupy your mind and keep those pesky worrisome thoughts at bay.

6. **iBreathe:** As an Apple-exclusive app, iBreathe is designed to help someone learn breathing techniques for anxiety management. It's useful for people needing a better night's sleep, as well as those who are learning to meditate.

7. **Mindshift:** Even though this app offers various types of support for many forms of anxiety, including phobias, OCD, and social anxiety, to name a few, each approach is

specific and targeted. It makes finding solutions much easier.

8. **Sanvello:** As a wellness app, Sanvello focuses on improving a person's life in all aspects. With the ability to log diet and exercise, as well as current feelings and moods, this app works on the whole of you and not just the mental health part. It also offers a search tool enabling people to find common anxieties and re-examine them so they can attempt to correct their stress and anxiety in the moment. This makes progress more apparent and inspiring.

UPCOMING INNOVATIONS TO MANAGE ANXIETY

While technology has come a long way in helping people manage their anxiety, your phone might get even smarter in the years to come. The researchers at the Institute of Business Administration and the Simon Fraser University have created a smartphone powered by artificial intelligence that can detect anxious behaviors with over 90% accuracy. The AI is used to observe a person's behavior as they go about their day, catching frequencies and instances of anxious activities.

It isn't just our phones that are moving beyond the expectations of health management, but researchers from the University of Illinois Chicago are studying gene editing for anxiety and alcohol use disorder. The link between binge drinking in adolescence and later in life anxiety is now being seen as an editable part of DNA. Only time will tell what advancements in health the medical professionals will be able to implement.

Personal Story

Lena had bouts of anxiety from her various phobias all throughout her twenties. She was racked with mental health illnesses: anxiety and agoraphobia the most. These two ailments would keep her up at night, and she found herself running on low energy each morning. To make things worse, she became irritable and emotional, which led to panic attacks.

When a friend noticed Lena's anxiety had been causing more and more problems in her life, she told Lena about a device called the Sensate 2, something she'd read about in a mindfulness magazine. Lena decided to give it a try and has never been more grateful.

The Sensate 2 is a little oval device that vibrates a purring sound, and it is meant to sit on your chest. The sound is like a chant or a hum that targets the vagus nerve, the very one that is responsible for initiating our fight or flight response. By supplying this nerve with a boost of rhythmic frequency, a person can reduce their stress and effectively lower their anxiety by a good measure.

Lena tried the device for a while, soon finding that her stress levels were indeed lower. This little technological breakthrough has continued to help Lena to this day, allowing her to regain control of some of her unwanted fears involving phobias and the worries that came with illness anxiety.

WHAT HAVE WE LEARNED

With the help of technology, there are many new treatments and improved methods for handling stress and anxiety.

- Social media and internet use can wear us out both physically and mentally. It's important to take frequent breaks and monitor your mood to know when enough is enough.
- Virtual reality can be used as a form of CBT to help reduce certain types of anxiety.
- Chatbots are effective in self-care as virtual friends that help us work through the things causing some of our anxiety and depression.
- Other helpful apps include Calm, iBreathe, Headspace, Sanvello, and others. There are some apps meant specifically to connect with a therapist as well.
- New innovations are on their way in the world of mental health improvement, including the possibility to edit genes and remove some forms of anxiety altogether.

MOVING AHEAD

Technology has its ups and downs, but when used correctly, it can guide us and connect us with the right form of anxiety care. Moving away from technology leads us to other, more alternative and natural forms of care that may bring our anxiety down for good.

Join me in the following chapter as we take a deeper look at some alternative anxiety treatments. These will bring us closer to being mindful and relaxed as we connect with nature, a healthy diet, and proper, positive activities.

CHAPTER 6

ALTERNATIVE ANXIETY BUSTERS

Medicine and therapy aren't the only ways to handle anxiety. There are many other alternative means of treatment, including dietary changes, herbal remedies, and other natural ways to reduce stress and thereby lower anxiety. Some people may want to choose a less invasive form of treatment and use supplements and herbal remedies rather than harsh chemical-based medications. Sometimes this is the first step in treating anxiety, and it can work for many people with the right amount of diligence.

Let's start by examining some treatments many people are turning to nowadays for more natural solutions to their troubles. Some of these can be done in the privacy of your own home, while others may need a professional to help.

NATURAL TREATMENTS FOR ANXIETY

Natural treatments that can help your anxiety and stress include things such as massage, acupuncture, support companions, light therapy, and cupping. As we go through these topics, keep in mind that some of them must be performed by a licensed professional, while others can be utilized in the comforts of your own home on your own time.

Acupuncture

As an ancient Chinese therapy that has been used for thousands of years, acupuncture is more popular than ever in the treatment of anxiety. This is especially true for people who want to use a method that is less harmful to the body, such as the side effects associated with medications. With acupuncture, a professional places very small, thin needles onto the pressure points throughout your body. It is believed that doing so will reduce your pain, anxiety, and stress associated throughout the body's diverse systems.

Massage

Massage therapy is well known to help alleviate stress throughout the body, and it is most commonly used for muscles and deep tissue aches. When visiting a massage therapist, also known as a masseuse, a licensed professional will perform a specific massage to help alleviate all types of stress. Various types of massages are available, including shiatsu, trigger point therapy, Swedish massage, and sports massage. With each of these types of massages, the technique may vary slightly, but the integral is to relax the muscles from being so tense that once we are faced with anxiety, we have no room left to tolerate the stress of the moment. When we carry extra tension in our muscles, we are already at our limit, which means that anxiety hits us almost instantly. When we are relaxed during stressful times, we are able to handle that anxiety much easier and prevent it from boiling over.

Combining massage therapy with other techniques, such as CBT, can allow us to face our heaviest forms of anxiety with a clear head and a more relaxed body.

Companion Therapy/Animal-Assisted Therapy

In the field of mental health, using support animals is no surprise in our modern world. It seems that everywhere we go, there is somebody who has a special needs companion with them, most often in the form of a dog. This may have begun as a way to help people with physical disabilities, but it has become a beloved form of mental health therapy as well. In addition to dogs, some people use cats and horses as well to allow them to face their toughest times without feeling alone.

Some therapy options will utilize animals during therapy sessions, but many people find that the benefits are overwhelmingly good, and they choose to go on to get their own service animal to keep them company throughout every moment of their lives. These animals are known to help people feel less lonely and to raise self-esteem so that confidence begins to grow. When we feel more confident about ourselves, it's easy to see how we can start to shine and embrace who we are instead of focusing on our faults and flaws. This can lower our anxiety exponentially and can create positive situations that were once overwhelmingly negative.

Light Therapy

Along with these common forms of therapy, there are also some lesser-known therapy options. One of these forms is light therapy, which is based on the fact that our bodies require sunlight to operate properly. Just like how people sometimes get the winter blues, which happens because our bodies are not receiving enough sunlight during the winter, we can reverse the effects of depression and stress by getting into the sun more often.

The sun provides our bodies with vitamin D, which is important for a plethora of health reasons, and it also allows us to feel happier overall. Aside from this vitamin, not getting enough sun in your life can also lead to Alzheimer's disease, asthma, and hypertension, to name a few. Light therapy is also known to help reduce migraines, heal wounds faster, and stabilize moods. Some forms of light therapy are artificial, allowing us to use this form of therapy year-round at any time of the day.

Wet Cupping

This might very well be the latest trend in Hollywood, but wet cupping is a therapy long rooted in history throughout the ancient world. People from the civilizations of ancient Egypt to Greece to the Chinese and Tibetan cultures have used wet cupping to increase blood circulation and relieve the tension in the muscles.

Wet cupping is also believed to balance the yin and yang throughout the body. These are the positive and negative forces within us, and by creating balance between them, it is believed that we can boost our immune systems, reduce pain and stress, and become our truest selves. This type of therapy can achieve many things, such as reducing inflammation and strengthening pain thresholds. It is no wonder that many people are trying out this ancient form of therapy to reduce stress levels and alleviate the tension throughout the body. It is also believed to help the lymphatic system, which is directly involved in handling toxins and inflammation.

With cupping, we find various forms of it available. Dry cupping uses suction only, whereas wet cupping may also involve bleeding in a controlled, supervised fashion. With running cupping, a massage therapist will apply oil to the body and then move the suction cups around rhythmically. Finally, flash cupping is when the suction is placed and released quickly across the body.

This form of muscle relaxation therapy is widely used in orthopedics and sports medicine. It can specifically help treat back pain, headaches, joint pain, and arthritis.

Wet Cupping in Islamic Tradition (Hijama)

When we talk about wet cupping in the Islamic faith, we are specifically referring to hijama. With this practice, wet cupping is paired with the recitation of the Quran, and the hijama practitioner should have done their wudu (ablution) during the procedure. Hijama is a highly spiritual experience that Muslims practice in order to remove toxic blood and acids from the body. This is an ancient form of healing that works not only on the body but also on the mind.

The Prophet Muhammad (Peace be upon him) was taught by the angels the method of wet cupping (hijama) as it is known in the Islamic faith.

"Glory to He Who took His servant for a journey by night from the most sacred mosque to the farthest mosque, whose precincts We blessed, in order that We might show him some of Our signs: for He is the One Who hears and sees [all things]" (Quran 17:1).

"I did not pass by an Angel from the Angels on the Night Journey except that they all said to me; 'Upon you is cupping (hijama), O Muhammad'" (Sahih; Sunan Ibn Majah °3477).

The Prophet Muhammad (Peace be upon him) made known that hijama was the best of all medicines available. It has long since been valued and used in various cultures throughout history. The Egyptians documented its use as far back as 1550 BCE. In addition, China has evidence of cupping being implemented over 5,000 years ago.

Hijama also helps to get the body to a normal state. It lifts and removes the acidity in the body and can create balance. The toxins in the blood that are causing it to remain stagnant and affect your mind and mood will only worsen over time. Hijama is the way to clear these toxins.

It is no wonder hijama is so beloved throughout the world. With everyone from religious devotees to celebrities practicing it, it is easy to see just how beneficial it can be. With documentation in the areas of circulation, fertility, pain relief, detoxification, and boosting the immune system, hijama is a proven method of cleansing from the inside out.

Hijama is also a perfect way to heal the mind and soul. It is relaxing and deeply spiritual, which helps to ease the mind of troubles, and removes anxiety and depression. It is known that the Prophet Muhammad (Peace be upon him) asked for hijama to be done on his own head for the removal of black magic. The best and most effective of all cures is possible when this is performed correctly.

The body has nine sunnah points, which are the places where the Prophet instructed for hijama. Sunnah, which is Arabic for "habitual practice of the Prophet," is also spelled Sunna. It is the body of traditional social and legal custom and practice of the Islamic community. Along with the Qur'ān (the Holy book of Islam) and Hadith (recorded sayings of the Prophet Muhammad), it is a major source of Shari'ah, or Islamic law. Traditional practice targets the upper back, which is where the heart, lungs, brain, and spine sunnah points are located. Hijama is also used to open and detoxify the main arteries throughout the body.

For a healthy person, hijama is needed only a few times throughout the year. For others who are facing serious illnesses, it can be done more often. The normal means is considered a hijama detox, and it is seen as a form of maintenance, both physically and mentally. According to Hadith, which is a collection of sayings by the Prophet Muhammad (PBUH) that accounts for his daily practice, there are also sacred sunnah days for hijama to be performed. The 17th, 19th, and 21st days of an Islamic lunar month are said to carry heavier results. If hijama is done on these days, then it is believed all diseases will be cured.

The prophet Muhammad was known to hold a practitioner of hijama in high regard.

"If there is anything good in the medicines with which you treat yourselves, it is in the incision of the hijama therapist, or a drink of honey...." (Muslim °2205)

In the spirit of this, it is revered as a Muslim to learn hijama and to perform it professionally for others. Because of this, a practitioner can expect to treat and possibly cure the types of ailments that modern medicine cannot. They can also help to bring the practice of hijama into the modern traditions of Islam, as well as earn a career that brings much satisfaction and spiritual rewards.

Celebrities who have experienced hijama include actresses Gwyneth Paltrow and Jennifer Anniston, singer Justin Bieber, and Olympic swimmer Michael Phelps.

Aside from using physical therapies, we must also pay attention to our diet when we are looking to reduce stress.

FOODS THAT MAY HELP REDUCE SYMPTOMS

A well-balanced diet consisting of wholesome, clean foods is always a good bet when dealing with mental or physical ailments. Some things seem like common sense, such as incorporating fresh fruits and dark green vegetables. In addition, we all know to choose whole grains over processed items and to pick protein sources that are lean and beneficial for our hearts. There are a few other quality items that can help reduce your anxiety and stress too.

Blueberries

Packed with an amazing array of antioxidants and vitamins, blueberries are one of nature's superfoods. It is believed that our bodies will crave vitamin C when we are feeling stressed out. This is because vitamin C is able to repair the cells in our bodies from the damage we incur during anxious bouts. To be proactive, we can eat plenty of fresh fruits that contain vitamin C, as well as other nutrients, to help prepare our bodies for moments of high stress and intense anxiety. These can help us rebound faster as we quickly get to feeling more like ourselves.

Fish

With omega-3 fatty acids and lean protein, fish can help our bodies and brains function as they should. This means we can avoid feeling overly stressed and instead handle the hurdles that come our way with ease and grace. When we are well nourished, we are stronger both mentally and physically, and these essential fatty acids help us to fight inflammation and regulate hormones.

Nuts and Seeds

Nuts and seeds have plenty of positive nutrients for our bodies, and some of them include anxiety-fighting substances such as magnesium, omega-3 fatty acids, and vitamin E. With inadequate levels of vitamin E, we may find that our moods are not stabilized. Some nuts and seeds, such as pumpkin seeds, also contain zinc, which can promote positive nerve and brain development that is directly involved in the processes of our emotions.

Legumes

The legume family, which includes beans and peas, is well known for providing protein, iron, and fiber to our diets. They also contain tryptophan, an amino acid that works to release serotonin and helps us relax and feel good. Tryptophan is often found in foods with high levels of protein, including all members of the legume family, and also nuts, oats, eggs, and dairy.

Fermented Foods

These items, such as yogurt and Kefir, are full of probiotics, and those things can help to fight against the unwanted bacteria in our guts. When our digestion is not properly managed, it can cause us several types of stress. But thankfully, it takes little time to get our diet back on track. In addition to probiotics, certain chemicals in our foods can help lower our stress and anxiety.

Dark Chocolate

If you've ever wanted a reason to eat chocolate, battling your anxiety is the best one yet. Because of the high content of trypto-phan in dark chocolate, you can expect your body to increase serotonin simply by indulging in a few pieces. Serotonin is the hormone in the body that allows us to feel good, optimistic, and find satisfaction.

Green Tea

Adding a cup of green tea to your daily routine will add the amino acid L-theanine, which is believed to lower stress levels. This amino acid is also promising at reducing anxiety and helping us to feel relaxed. Remember that when we begin our day relaxed, we are able to take on the things that may otherwise weigh us down.

Turmeric

Curcumin, which is a compound found in turmeric, is used in the treatment of depression and anxiety. This is very similar to the chemicals in chocolate as to how it can enhance serotonin, but it also boosts dopamine, which plays a pivotal role in pleasure and motivation. Many people like to add turmeric to their smoothies in the morning to enhance their "feel good" mood for the day.

When we look at these ingredients separately, it's easy to see why so many people are adding these superfoods to their daily routine in an effort to balance their mental state and mood, as well as build their immunity to environmental stresses.

The foods we eat are highly important because we must eat to survive. But we can also add in herbal remedies to further enhance our mental health and find that relaxed state of mind we wish so badly to achieve.

HERBAL REMEDIES

Herbs have long been used to heal the body and mind. In ancient times, herbal remedies were the medicine, and some cultures still swear by them to this day. It is the principles founded by the ancients that paved the way for modern medicine, and some herbs are still used presently for their healing properties.

It is important to know that each herb here may affect an individual in adverse ways. Before trying something new, always consult your physician and discuss any concerns or thoughts you have. Finding a solution to your mental health takes time, and you must be open to talking to a professional to get the right treatment. The last thing you want is to feel more anxious or fearful because of using something unfamiliar or not right for you.

Ashwagandha (Withania somnifera)

This herb is an adaptogen, which is a pharmaceutical that may be anti-fatigue, antidepressant, and neuroprotective. This means ashwagandha is able to help reduce stress levels as well as anxiety.

Chamomile (Matricaria recutita)

This herb is known mostly for being used in tea as a way to calm one down before sleep. Because of its relaxation properties, it is perfect for reducing anxiety. Chamomile is also wonderful for helping skin problems, settling upset stomachs, easing indigestion, and also acts as an anti-inflammatory.

Hops (Humulus lupulus)

This herb is well known for being an ingredient in beer, but because it has sedative properties, it is excellent at helping people with anxiety. They even help with tense nerves, insomnia, and depression. Hops have been used since the 1500s for various reasons, and among them, hops can improve the libido and enhance the health of the heart.

Kava (Piper methysticum)

Another herb used in traditional cultural practices, kava, as the Pacific Islanders know it, is used ceremonially for relaxation. It is also believed to protect neurons and reduce pain. These can easily help to reduce anxiety and make a person feel more comfortable.

Lavender (Lavandula angustifolia)

Perhaps the most widely known herb for stress, lavender is used in hundreds of items, from soaps to lip balms to shampoo. Lavender is excellent for helping to fight insomnia, headaches, and anxiety. The herb is also believed to boost the mood and help with minor skin issues.

Lemon Balm (Melissa officinalis)

Often used to help boost the mood and improve cognition, lemon balm is a herb used all across the globe. This herb is great at reducing stress and anxiety and can also aid in digestive issues.

St. John's Wort (Hypericum perforatum)

This herb is widely known for helping the mood stabilize, mostly by reducing the symptoms of depression. St. John's Wort is also known to reduce stress hormones and help lower levels of inflammation.

Valerian (Valeriana officinalis)

Similar to chamomile, valerian is often seen as a tea. It is generally used to combat stress and anxiety, and it is also known to offer sedative properties. With the nickname of "nature's valium," it's no wonder that valerian is used to promote relaxation and proper sleep.

SUPPLEMENTS

Aside from using herbal supplements, there are other items that we can add to our dietary routine to enhance our moods and lessen the anxiety we feel each day.

GABA

As a neurotransmitter and amino acid, gamma-aminobutyric acid helps to produce serotonin in the brain. It is a highly powerful neurotransmitter that can help to regulate the way we feel good about certain things, as well as how we relax.

Vitamin D

Lacking proper levels of vitamin D can be associated with fatigue, muscle and joint pain, and weight gain. And because of the afore-mentioned winter blues, we already know that low levels of vitamin D are associated with anxiety and depression. Not only will adding a vitamin D supplement to your diet help you fight the fatigue and depression you feel from low levels, but it can also help you absorb calcium which is vital to strengthening our bones. The thing about calcium is that our bodies cannot put it to use unless it is properly absorbed, which is why vitamin D is so vital.

Vitamin B Complex

This set of vitamins is important for our nervous system to function properly, but they also aid in our mental health. The vitamin B complex group is responsible for helping us retain energy and cognition, but they also promote a positive mood and stress management.

Magnesium

As a mineral, magnesium is important for aiding nearly every part of the body, including mental abilities. Because of this, it is believed that magnesium can help alleviate symptoms of anxiety. Thankfully, this mineral is found in abundance in some of the healthy foods we should incorporate into our diets, to begin with. Spinach, almonds, dark chocolate, and whole wheat are a few of the items that contain magnesium.

L-Theanine

This is an amino acid that is proven to lower our stress levels and help us relax. Along with this, L-theanine can also help us focus better. Common in supplements, this amino acid is often paired with GABA to better enhance the way we handle anxiety.

Multivitamins

A mix of multivitamins is sure to help anyone obtain better health. Sometimes we are low in certain nutrients and are unsure of where to start, so by using multivitamins on a daily basis, we can expect to feel better physically and mentally in little time. Multivitamins will typically contain the main vitamins needed to enhance our focus, ease our digestion, and make us better equipped to handle anxiety.

Omega-3 Fatty Acids

These oils are typically found in fish and are crucial to the brain and the nervous system. They help with cognition, and they can alleviate the various symptoms associated with depression.

WHAT HAVE WE LEARNED

In this chapter, we've discussed the various ways you can address your mental health struggles with natural remedies. Of these, we included the following information:

- Massage therapy is a great way to release tension in the muscles and allow us to combat daily anxiety.
- Wet cupping is a technique used to help enhance circulation and promote muscle relaxation.
- Hijama cupping is the Islamic version of wet cupping to remove toxins and acids from the body, which also helps dispel anxiety and depression.
- A balanced diet consisting of nutritional plant-based foods and lean proteins can help provide the right vitamins and minerals to alleviate stress and anxiety.
- Certain herbal remedies are known to directly impact our stress and can boost the way our bodies react to anxiety in a more positive way.
- Sometimes our bodies lack certain vitamins and minerals, and once they are included in the form of supplements, we can begin to feel better or better anxiety in little time.

MOVING AHEAD

Now that we've learned how to help reduce anxiety on a natural level with things you can do on your own, let's look at how other people can help us in our fight. Up until now, we've trusted technology, professionals, and the occasional massage therapist to wet cupping/hijama experts, but we also have our loving family and support system. These people are with us every day, and they know us like we know ourselves. They just might be the impact we need to overcome some forms of anxiety.

It's important to remember that even when we feel entirely alone, we never truly are. There is always someone wanting to help and see you succeed. And once you know how they can assist you, it's possible you can help others too. And that is the best recovery of all.

CHAPTER 7

ON THE OTHER SIDE: HELPING A LOVED ONE WITH ANXIETY

Sometimes the anxiety that we face in life isn't our own. It can be difficult to know how to act and what to say to someone who's going through anxiety or an episode of depression. We want to show our love and support to the people in our lives who matter most to us, and the last thing we want to do is to make their troubles worse.

There is an old saying, "Sticks and stones may break my bones, but words can never hurt me." But it may not be true after all. It is important to understand that our words carry weight. The things we say to each other matter a lot, and they can strike a deep chord with our emotions. There are scientific studies to show just how our words can affect us on a deep psychological level. We must be careful with how we approach people in our everyday situations, but also, and more especially, when people are going through difficult times. Some of the things we say can be positive and uplifting, whereas others can bring negative energy into a person's life. Our interactions with others can greatly influence their future choices and behaviors, and that means that we are essentially helping or hurting other people long after our interactions are over.

We truly must be aware of the energy we give off in any given situation, even if it does not involve anxiety or depression. We should always be cautious and sensitive when we choose our words and be kind and sincere where necessary.

These truths are important from childhood on. Some studies have proven that children with higher rates of negative self-talk and low self-esteem are more likely to suffer from anxiety. In addition, when we teach our children to believe a certain way, it can either boost their positive self-image or greatly hinder their confidence.

Because of the way our brains work, it is known that when we hear negative things, whether it be an insult to our own person or a tragic event happening around the world, we feel those things deeply in our hearts. We feel sympathy and compassion toward the people who must experience those hardships, and for ourselves, we feel belittled, embarrassed, and even worthless.

In any case, remember to choose your words carefully and to be kind to others, no matter what you may think or feel in the moment. We can never truly understand what it is like to be in the other person's shoes, so in the least, we must be compassionate to their personal struggles so that one day they can be considerate of ours.

WHAT TO SAY TO THOSE SUFFERING WITH ANXIETY

There are many times when a person intends to be polite and considerate, but in reality, they only end up making the situation worse. As we've discussed, we can never truly understand what it feels like to live the other person's life. We don't understand why they are short-tempered or have mood swings, and more often than not, they will have a very good reason for these bad behaviors and attitudes. It is not up to us to judge or offer advice unless we are asked for it, but as friends and family of the people we care about, we must be there to support them through their difficulties.

These behaviors are often seen as toxic behaviors, ones that are negative in nature and will often push people away. Someone may be impolite to you, or they might say things they wouldn't normally say, and it is important to remember that something has happened to them to make them behave this way. Good-natured people will not be cruel for no reason. It doesn't excuse the behavior, and it must be corrected, but as someone who cares about their family and friends, you should want to do everything you can to make the person feel better as they conquer their fears and anxiety. The end goal with any type of behavior correction is to help the person learn from their mistakes and overcome whatever it is that is holding them back.

The toxic behavior we discuss here is often attributed to anxiety and depression. When people do not feel like themselves, they lash out at others simply because they may be embarrassed or feel less than worthy. Another person in their lives may have made them feel this way just because of something that was said. Without taking the time to understand what is truly going on in this person's life, no real improvements can be made. It can be easy to yell at each other and name faults. But taking the easy way out will not achieve the results you seek.

Things You Should Say

If you have a friend or a family member who is dealing with anxiety or depression, especially if they are displaying a cry for help through their toxic behavior, then you must take the time to understand what has triggered this terrible feeling in your friend or family member. Only then can you truly help, and that is where the real results occur.

- What can I do to help you?
- I am here for you. You are not alone.
- Would it help if I just sat here with you and listened?
- Do you want to do something to take your mind off of things?
- I love you, and I am always here for you, no matter what is going on.
- Do you want me to come over?
- Are you looking for advice, or would you rather I just listen?

These things open the door for you to help, but they don't impose your advice or judgment. This can allow your friend or family member to feel comfortable speaking with you and knowing you are there to support them, no matter what they are going through.

Things You Should Not Say

Just as there are things you can say to support your friend, there are several that you should avoid. These are the types of things most people will instinctively think of saying, and even if your heart is in the right place, you could actually do more harm than good. The last thing you want is to make your friend feel as though they are making something big out of nothing or feeling normal anxiety when in reality, they might need professional help.

- You'll get over it. Just snap out of it.
- I know, that makes me feel really anxious too.
- Have you tried . . .?
- There's no reason to panic.

- Everyone gets stressed sometimes. This is completely normal.
- Just stop worrying, and you'll feel so much better.
- Other people have it much worse than you.
- Are you going through this again?
- You're just overreacting.
- Weren't you just fine a minute ago?

As you can see, these types of statements and questions only make a person feel doubtful and more nervous. Instead of offering support and love, you will actually end up making the person feel like they are the only one in the world going through something like this. For an anxious person, this can be the worst thing ever. Sometimes when people deal with anxiety, it can get to the point where they simply fear the inevitable panic attack that comes with their anxiety. As Franklin D. Roosevelt so famously put, "The only thing to fear is fear itself."

This often goes hand in hand with something I learned from being a mother. When a child is young and falls and hurts themselves, your first instinct is to ask them if they're okay. Unfortunately, this only puts the idea in their minds that they may not be okay. Rather than leaving this to a young and undeveloped mind who has now experienced something fearful and possibly painful, it's much better to comfort them with a statement like, "I'm right here with you. Everything is okay." This shows a young child that they are not alone and that the things they're going through are not as epic as they might first imagine.

OTHER WAYS YOU CAN HELP

If you feel as though you would like to do more for your friend or family member, and especially if you can see they are hurting but do not ask for help or are reluctant to cooperate, there are other things you can do to make them feel at ease.

Get Curious

If you have not experienced anxiety or depression in a way that you see in your friend, then the first thing you must do is to become more curious about what their anxiety is and how it can be addressed. Do your research and ask questions about the different types of symptoms and struggles people with anxiety will go through. Even when you are visiting with your physician, it is an opportunity to ask a question about a loved one. Sometimes seeking advice is difficult for someone who is going through anxiety or depression, especially because in the moment when you feel those symptoms come on, it can be incredibly hard to put into words all the feelings and emotions that come with panic.

Taking the time to understand what it is your friend is experiencing is a major step in the right direction. Not only will it show them that you care about them and are willing to do whatever it takes to help them feel better, but you will be better prepared for dealing with anxiety with other people in your life and even yourself if the occasion arises.

Show Your Care and Concern

Showing compassion toward the people you care about is as easy as being patient. The last thing you want to do is make a person with anxiety feel as though they are rushed and must immediately come up with explanations and solutions to their problems. They need to be comforted and understood, which can only happen with time. By showing that you care and are concerned about their overall well-being, you are helping them to heal with each interaction you have.

When your friend is dealing with something that is causing them anxiety, sometimes the only thing you can do is sit by their side and listen to them. Well, not everybody has experienced anxiety to the point of panic, and it is true that we have all dealt with something that has brought us suffering in our lives. Even if it's a small thing, we understand what it means to be listened to and to be comforted. If you were to experience the type of daily struggle that comes with anxiety, then you would know that your friend needs a shoulder to lean on more than ever.

Validate Their Experiences and Emotions

This goes hand in hand with taking time to listen and comfort your friend. You don't want to go so far as to say that everyone feels anxiety, that it's completely normal, and that they should get over their fears. But you do want to let them know that they have every right to feel the way they are feeling. If you have experienced anxiety, you can discuss your struggles and anything that has helped you along the way. Again, pay attention to how your friend is acting and responding to this discussion because you do not want to impose your judgment or advice unless it is asked for.

Help Them to Feel Safe

A lot of different fears that turn into anxiety stem from feeling unsafe. At its root, anxiety is a fear we feel we cannot overcome or control. Some people may experience anxiety when on a plane or on a boat, and in this example, it is completely rational to feel fearful. You can help your friend by talking them through the moment and showing them that things are OK and that they are safe at your side. In addition, you can also discuss things with your friend before an event or when other occasions arise to help them prepare. You can discuss different CBT methods and other calming things, such as breathing techniques, exercise options, and dietary changes that may help them feel more at ease.

Talk Them through a Visualization

This is where you can assist your friend with one of those CBT methods, helping them to cope with their anxiety, so they are less likely to feel the heavy struggles that come with it. The two of you can devise a make-believe session where you walk through a situation that would normally cause your friend anxiety. Practicing little by little, you can help your friend feel more at ease with the situation they may be avoiding due to their fears. Eventually, your friend will be able to face their fear with more confidence and positivity, and they will be grateful to you for being patient and considerate of how they are feeling.

Use Mindful Awareness

This is another tactic we have covered in our treatments chapter. Being mindful means being completely grounded in your current reality. You can be mindful of the people around you, the environment you're in, and everything else that makes up the reality you exist within. One incredibly helpful way to remain mindful during an episode of anxiety is to use your senses to connect with the world around you. This is a trick you can practice with your friend in a very comfortable environment where there are no anxiety triggers to cause fear.

Just like the 3–3–3 method, where we pay attention to three different things in our environment that pertain to three different senses, we can use mindful techniques to keep us in the present. And remember, doing this pulls us away from those thoughts we have that often seem to take over our rational minds. These runaway thoughts are exactly those things that create the fear and panic we dread so much.

One particular mindful method I enjoy using is to simply name one thing from each of the five senses. This is a quick response that brings me entirely into the real world and out of my mind. Going through each of the senses, pull one thing from your environment and name it out loud. This is such a quick and simple technique that it can be done anytime and in any place, and it definitely helps when you have a friend in need. When the two of you can practice this together or even use it during a situation when the friend is feeling anxious, it is almost like reaffirming the environment through two sets of eyes, making the reality even more so.

Put Things into Perspective

Putting things into perspective is when we compare something we are dealing with, with something similar to get a clearer picture of the overall situation. We can use this to overcome moments of anxiety by showing ourselves that we are not truly dealing with something as horrible as our minds are making it out to be. This can help someone close to you deal with their anxiety as well, and your help goes to show that you are there for them and that they are not facing their struggles alone.

You can, for example, use an instance of a time that did not cause anxiety and compare it to a similar time that did. You can look at these two different situations with your friend to show them that even though they are fearful of something bad happening, things did truly work out fine for them. This can be useful in overcoming past trauma anxiety. Let's say your friend was in a terrible car accident, and now when they get in a car, they feel a little rush of panic. You can help by talking to them about all the times they have been in a car, and everything went fine. You can comfort them by telling them that there is plenty they can do while driving, such as keeping their distance, wearing a seatbelt, being alert, and not having distractions. And you can also discuss how even if those things did not go as planned and a car accident did happen, your friend is okay now, they have healed from that moment, and time has continued to move forward.

A Personal Story

As a person who has dealt with anxiety their whole life, Iman was certain that her feelings were completely normal. Over time, however, she discovered that her anxiety was causing panic and that she was spending days upon days feeling strung out and having headaches. At one point, she decided enough was enough and that she needed to do her own research about her feelings and emotions so that she could gain control over her life. What she found was an interesting collection of advice that she wished she had years ago. Of that advice, these were her key takeaways:

Always Listen to Your Intuition

We have gut feelings about everything, and even though some of us are not the best at reading people and environments, we still must pay attention to how we feel when we are in the middle of a situation. If you're about to do something and you feel a sort of dread or panic coming on, don't ignore that feeling. It doesn't mean that you need to feed into your anxiety and begin believing that all your fears are justified, but it does mean that whatever you are dealing with is causing you stress and uncertainty. And those are things that none of us want to deal with because they linger for hours even after the situation is over.

Just Be Good Enough

No one is perfect. No matter what you perceive or what you think you believe about someone else, perfection is an illusion. When we fight to obtain perfection, we cause ourselves endless stress and agony. Some of these stresses cause anxiety and can lead to body shaming, low self-esteem, and self-rejection. No one will have a perfectly clean house that needs no repairs. No one will have perfect teeth or the leanest, most beautiful body. These things are simply unattainable, and the quicker we realize that, the sooner we can overcome some of the anxiety we impose upon ourselves.

Your Parents Are Doing the Best They Can

It's such a classical cliche to blame the parent for the child's struggles. Whether it happens or not in clinical psychology, it happens to be in every movie. What is your relationship with your mother? That happens to be a big one. But we must remember that it is our environment and our relationships that form who we are to this day. Yes, some people have awfully hard childhoods filled with trauma that may take a lifetime to overcome. But even so, we must remember that our parents and other caregivers have also shown us love and support. Feel that love and find it when you are struggling and let go of some of the things you hold as blame. And when you cannot find that comfort through a parental figure, as we all should, reach out to friends and other family members to relieve your stress and set your mind free.

Have Faith in Yourself

Taking a step backward or falling off the wagon is okay, but you must continue getting on your feet and fighting for that next step forward. Only you can push yourself, and only you can fight for what you want most. In time, with patience and diligence, you will discover who you truly are and how best to live your life. You must be kind to yourself first and love yourself unconditionally.

With these four pieces of advice, Iman was able to see herself in a different way. She came to understand that without knowing herself and loving herself, she wasn't able to be herself, and that was holding her back from achieving things in all aspects of her life. And this most definitely included overcoming some of her anxiety. More to the point, Iman discovered which of her friends were her true friends and which ones were only hindering her recovery. The friends that mattered the most stuck around and had the patience to help her work through her struggles and become her best self. Those friends were there to tell her that she was doing great, even when she doubted herself. They were there to listen when she was struggling, and they supported her intuition when she felt things were off. And in the end, as she felt she had finally regained control over her life and her emotions, she had not only found herself, but she had also found a network of people who would help and support her throughout the rest of her life.

WHAT HAVE WE LEARNED

Throughout this chapter, we've discussed how to help other people who are going through anxiety and depression. There are a few key points that will help your friends manage their anxiety and possibly even overcome some of their fears.

- Choosing your words carefully is important. Positive words can improve a person's life, whereas negative words can hinder them.
- Sometimes sitting there and listening to your friend is more important than offering any type of advice.
- We want to say things that help our friends know they are not alone and that we support them in whatever they are feeling.
- We should avoid telling our friends that they need to get over their fears and are overreacting. We never want to make them feel like they are a burden or that their fears are unfounded.
- The best way to help someone in need is to fully research the anxiety they are experiencing and then take the time to show that you care and want your friend to heal and feel better.

MOVING AHEAD

Now that we've discussed so many diverse aspects of anxiety and how it can be treated, especially how to help someone who is in need and trying to get help, we can look at the final piece of the puzzle to help us live a fulfilling and calm life. Studies show that living a spiritual life can exponentially improve a person's mental health. Knowing that there is a higher purpose for us and that we are not alone in our struggles and trials can greatly improve our self-confidence and mindfulness throughout every aspect of our lives.

Join me in the final chapter as we discuss faith and the role it can play in bringing you peace of mind.

CHAPTER 8

CONQUERING ANXIETY THROUGH FAITH

Throughout our lives, we are always searching for a place to belong. When we have religion and spirituality to back us and guide us through our lives, we are never alone and feel that we always belong somewhere. This type of comfort is something we cannot buy and own, but we can discover it for ourselves as we travel through life and become truer to who we are.

There have been studies proving that people with depression are often those who are not religious and who also lack good health. A 2005 study conducted in the San Francisco area found that religious people had better health and lower levels of depression. In addition, Dr. Harold G. Koenig of the Center for Spirituality, Theology and Health at Duke University found that religious people, on average, had fewer symptoms of depression. This was found through his research of ninety-three different studies on the topic.

Aside from having religion and spirituality in your life, it is also known that engaging in spiritual practices can help people handle their stress a lot easier than those who do not. Again, this is connected to how spirituality and religion give us a sense of purpose in life as they provide meaning for the behaviors and thoughts we have. Being spiritual and understanding your place in the universe can help you find support when you are lost and also provide help for those who need encouragement.

HOW FAITH HELPS YOU COPE WITH ANXIETY

There is evidence that having a higher purpose present in your life can help you handle stress in a much healthier way. Trusting in something that is beyond explanation might seem difficult for some, but once you allow that guiding light into your life, it can help to shoulder the burden of the many hardships we face throughout our lives. This can include illnesses, loss, financial strain, and broken relationships, for example. Of the various things faith can do for your life, the following are especially important:

- **Having faith in something greater than us all can provide meaning and purpose to your life.** Faith is about following something with your heart, and by doing this, we look at the big picture of things instead of focusing on the little details. This helps us get our minds out of our stresses, as it allows us to focus on what we are truly doing here in our lives.
- **Faith can strengthen your values that are affected by stress.** Our values are things such as providing sympathy and showing kindness to others. When we have faith in ourselves and our fellow peers, we act generously and show them compassion rather than anger and hostility. Faith forces us to see people for whom they could become rather than what they currently are. This is important because sometimes people are going through

unexplainable situations, and it will often have them
appearing toxic and showing the worst side of themselves.
With our faith, we can look past these things and see
people for the good of who they are.

- **Faith allows us to find hope as we accept ourselves and
our current situations.** With faith, not only are we
strengthened in our compassion for others, but we are also
hopeful of the good things that may come. Faith
encourages us to accept who we are and the environment
in which we live and to be positive about what we have
instead of focusing on the things we do not.

- **Faith brings us closer together as a community.** Because
we are kind and hopeful, we want to see others do well. We
want the people we interact with on a daily basis to be
happy and fulfilled, which means we offer our support and
become united as one.

- **Having faith can calm our hearts and minds.** Just as we
find meditation as a means to relieve stress, prayer
through faith also reduces stress and anxiety. Trusting in a
higher power to guide you and help you live your best life
can also bring joy and remove some of the sadness and
depression you may face.

Having faith is a beautiful thing for anyone's life and beneficial in
helping people live a more fulfilling and meaningful life. For
myself, my faith as a Muslim has helped me find meaning and
purpose in the simplest of things throughout my day. The Islamic
faith has guided me and taught me many values I hold dearly. As a
means to heal from anxiety, the Islamic faith is proven to help
people find peace.

ANXIETY IN ISLAMIC FAITH

A study published in the National Library of Medicine in 2022 suggests that religious practice in the Islamic faith has been beneficial to healing anxiety and helping to prevent depression. Depression could also happen because of excessive anxiety or the fear of something terrible happening. Because so many people have strayed from faith and decided to live their lives based on material possessions and pleasure-seeking goods, they have strayed from the meaning and purpose that faith offers. They've allowed themselves to go too far down a pathway that has led to uncertainty and instability. When we reach this point alone, and we find ourselves looking for answers and hoping for support, we only feel the fear that comes with an ambiguous world. Faith in Allah is the answer to finding that place you belong and never feeling alone again.

The practices that go along with the Islamic faith are highly beneficial in helping people overcome their psychological struggles and mental disorders. Listening to the Holy Quran and hearing the verses that explain forgiveness and compassion can help ease the mind and bring comfort to those who have only known pain. In the study that was published, the researchers focused mainly on the impact of RSAFI, which is remembrance and seeking Allah's forgiveness. The researchers wondered whether RSAFI had any impact on depression or anxiety, and they conducted their study with various groups over thirty different sessions, all of which took approximately fifteen weeks to complete.

With the different groups, researchers reviewed specific religious concepts such as seeking forgiveness, patience, spiritual values, and repentance, to name a few. The results showed that the test groups scored lower on anxiety and depression than the control groups. This went on to show that the Islamic faith's core principles and teachings helped people feel better about themselves and lower their stress levels.

THOSE WHO HAVE SUCCESSFULLY DEALT WITH ANXIETY IN ISLAM

As we have seen, celebrities, singers, actors, and countless other people of our time have dealt with anxiety in their own ways. Now we will see how the lives of the messengers of Allah, the true superstars of the universe, and some righteous people having a very high status in the eyes of Allah have been impacted by anxiety. Their life struggles, the difficulties they have faced, and the triumphs they gained through their faith are all here. Throughout history, Prophets and others alike have dealt with anxiety, and the Islamic faith has been there to help them rise above their fears.

Prophet Nuh (Noah) (Peace be upon him)

As the years went on, the people of Earth practiced idolatry. Allah saw the need for change, and so He sent Nuh (Peace be upon him) as a guide for his people. They needed to find the right path and to be righteous once again, grateful for the beauty and the splendor in Allah's world. Nuh was patient with the people, and he spoke eloquently about his Lord. He told the people to only worship Allah.

Nuh made it known that the Devil had distracted and deceived the people for far too long. It was time for a change. Nuh preached this message for over nine hundred years, and even though Nuh was met with arguments and disdain, he kept his faith. He taught of the need for Allah every hour of every day of his life.

With his relentless dedication to Allah, Nuh was mocked for his beliefs. He asked Allah, after growing tired and saddened from thinking his work was in vain, to destroy the nonbelievers across the face of the earth. Allah accepted the prayer and instructed Nuh (Peace be upon him) to build an ark. After the building was complete, the rains came, and the earth flooded. With his son and wife among the nonbelievers, Nuh cried out for his son to join him. He did not heed his call but instead sought refuge on a tall mountain. Nuh was distraught. He feared losing his family to the terrible flood and storm he had warned people about for years. The huge wave swept him away, frightening Nuh, filling him with anxiety and grief. He called upon God to show mercy.

"And Noah called upon his Lord and said, 'Oh my Lord! Verily, my son is of my family! And certainly, Your Promise is true, and You are the Most Just of the judges.'

Allah said, 'Oh Noah! Surely, he is not of your family; verily, his work is unrighteous, so ask not of Me that of which you have no knowledge! I admonish you, lest you be one of the ignorants.'

Noah said, 'Oh my Lord! I seek refuge with You from asking You that of which I have no knowledge. And unless You forgive me and have Mercy on me, I would indeed be one of the losers." (Quran: 11:45-47)

Imagine losing someone near and dear to you, and that you want that person to be guided, but he or she pays no heed. How would this make you feel? Losing someone so important. Although Noah's anxiety and grief of losing his son forever is beyond imagination, it is noteworthy that it did not affect his mannerism and sincerity towards Allah. He accepted the will of Allah without question.

Prophet Ibrahim (Abraham) (Peace be upon him)

Ibrahim tried to spread the word of Allah and, in doing so, found his own village to have many idols and figurines in place of their gods. Ibrahim destroyed the idols and explained that they could not protect themselves, so why then would the people worship them? The townspeople and their king, Nimrod of Babylon, ordered Ibrahim to be burned by fire. Ibrahim (Peace be upon him) was abandoned by those he saw as his greatest support, his family and his community, and loneliness overwhelmed him.

Loneliness is difficult when we are physically apart from those we love, but feeling isolated from the people we once trusted, especially while they surround us, is the worst type of loneliness. Ibrahim felt this form of loneliness, as his beloved community that once supported and adored him had turned against him. It is here that his faith was truly tested.

Ibrahim had always spoken to Allah about his father and how he revered him and praised him. And in Ibrahim's time of need, it wasn't just the community and his family who betrayed him; it was most especially his father. Imagine the pain of Ibrahim (Peace be upon him). This broke Ibrahim's heart more than anything. As he was stripped and placed into the catapult to be tossed into a fire, one that had been stoked for days upon days, heat spilling over and frightening the people, Ibrahim felt complete humiliation. Not a single onlooker showed sympathy. Not one person came to Ibrahim's aid.

During this moment, the angel Jibreel (Gabriel) (Alaihis salam) visited Ibrahim and asked if he wanted help. Instead of asking for his life to be spared, he said he wanted Allah to be pleased with him. He said, *"Hasbunallahu wa ni'mal wakeel. Allah is sufficient for us, and He is the best disposer of our affairs."*

Once again, what we learn is trust in Allah. Allah could not allow Ibrahim (Peace be upon him) to be executed, and so the fire did not burn him but was cool and peaceful. The people discovered that Ibrahim's God was powerful and good, and He had saved him from the flames. Alas, he was never alone! Allah had never once left his side.

Prophet Yunus (Jonah) (Peace be upon him)

Allah called upon Yunus (Peace be upon him) to spread his word to the city of Nineveh, but the people there would not listen. Yunus left and set out to sea discouraged, and a great storm began. The sailors believed their pagan gods were upset with them, and they decided to throw Yunus overboard after drawing a lot to appease them. An enormous whale swallowed Yunus (Peace be upon him) and took the Prophet deep into the darkness of the ocean. Yunus cried out to Allah that He is the only God, trusting his faith even when he felt no hope for his life. Quran says:

"And remember when the Man of the Whale stormed off from his city in a rage, thinking We would not restrain him. Then in the veils of darkness he cried out, La ilaha illa anta soub haa naka inni kuntu minaz-zalimeen. There is no god worthy of worship except You. Glory be to You! I have certainly done wrong." (Quran 21:87)

Allah answered by bringing the whale to the surface to spit Yunus out onto the beach. Allah takes more care of him under the burning sun by growing a plant that shades him. Upon recovery, Yunus (Peace be upon him) sees that his city has returned to Allah, and his mission is complete.

The lesson here is that Allah is always in control, and we must allow ourselves to trust in Him, no matter what. We can never truly know what effect our deeds will have on others until they are completed. We must always do things right and just and be kind and patient with others. Sympathy goes a long way in our world, especially knowing that people everywhere are dealing with their own troubles. We cannot simply be short-tempered and think only of ourselves in those times. No matter if we are witness to the weight of our words or not, we must always try to be good and do good. And remember that whatever darkness may surround you in your life, and you can't find a way out: do not hesitate to call out to God, telling Him that your faith lies in His power and that you trust in His mercy. Great and amazing things will come from Allah, and we need only trust.

Prophet Musa (Moses) (Peace be upon him)

Musa (Peace be upon him) was told by God to speak with Pharaoh for the release of the Israelites. Musa showed the Pharaoh that his God is the one true God, but the Pharaoh was unphased. He trusted in his wealth and power, things of the material world, ones that caused many of his citizens to suffer, want, horde, and flaunt. Musa was able to convince the Pharaoh's magicians that he was authentic in his abilities because his God was true and held high strength. Musa tried to free the Israelites against Pharaoh's will, so he, along with his army, chased after Musa and the Israelites, still believing him to be the wrong. Musa fled Egypt with his people, meeting the Red Sea, where many doubted the power of the Almighty Allah. They thought they'd meet their demise for sure. Musa was confident, striking the water with his staff, parting the sea in half.

"Indeed, we are to be overtaken!"

Musa (Peace be upon him) did not lose his faith for one second. His trust in Allah kept his fears and worries at bay. Though the men and women around Musa were frightened and panicked,

Musa let go of his anxiety and trusted only in Allah. He knew that God was sufficient for his survival.

"No! Indeed, with me is my Lord; He will guide me.

Then We inspired to Moses, "Strike with your staff the sea," and it parted, and each portion was like a great towering mountain.

And We advanced thereto the pursuers.

And We saved Moses and those with him, all together.

Then We drowned the others.

Indeed, in that is a sign, but most of them were not to be believers." (Quran 26:61-67)

With Musa's faith and the guidance of Allah, the sea stayed wide open for the Israelites to escape. They arrived at the opposite shore unharmed, and when the Pharaoh and his men tried to pursue Musa (Peace be upon him) and the Israelites, they were swept away and killed.

The lesson in this story is that we must never allow our doubts and fears to conquer us but allow our faith to free us from the burdens of losing hope. With Allah, hope is never lost. He went to great lengths to keep his promise to Musa and save the Children of Israel. If Allah is able to part the sea to save those who trust in Him, what else is possible when we give Him our faith? Hope and faith provide us with all we need when it comes to letting go of the fears and stresses that are holding us back. Instead of believing the worst is sure to happen, know that Allah is near and with you and can resolve all that ails you if you only ask.

Asiyah, Wife of the Pharaoh

The same Pharaoh who challenged Musa (Peace be upon him) also challenged his own wife, Asiyah bint Muzaahim (May Allah be pleased with her), who took care of Prophet Musa as her son. Lady Asiyah was witness to the terrible tyranny of the Pharaoh, but in one such instance, she saw the resolve and courage of a woman who faced death. The woman kept to her faith, knowing the next life was more beautiful and had no suffering like this world. Lady Asiyah (May Allah be pleased with her), found strength in the woman's actions, and she told her husband she did not believe him to be a god but that she believed in the one true God, Allah. Even though the Pharaoh took Asiyah to the desert, starved, and stripped her, she kept her faith. She asked Allah to build her a house near Him, in the paradise of His heaven. In response to her Dua (supplication), Allah opened the skies and allowed her to see what was waiting for her in Paradise, and she laughed in joy at this. Before the Pharaoh could have her killed, Allah took Asiyah's soul.

It is clear that the lesson here is that no pain or suffering should ever be greater than one's desire to connect with Allah. Asiyah's devotion and faith to Allah not only stayed true through her oppressive marriage and suffering but in the end, she asked not for a place in paradise but a place near to her Lord. She wanted the comforts of being in His presence more than the comforts of a sublime residence in heaven. She discovered the courage necessary to rise above her oppressors and keep her honor to her faith intact. Her life may have ended there in the desert, but she is elevated in Islam for having perfect faith and for choosing the one true God and the eternal bliss of His love. This rather than her husband, a man who sought nothing but power in a materialistic world of self-suffering.

Maryam (Mary), Mother of Esa (Jesus), Peace Be upon Them Both

As a devout woman of religion, Maryam (Peace be upon her) spent her youth and young adult life dedicated to Allah. Even though she had never been touched by a man, she became pregnant. The angel Jibreel (Gabriel) visited Maryam (Peace be upon her) and told her that she was to carry and birth the Prophet Esa (Jesus Peace be upon him). Because she was relentless in her faith and trusted in Allah, no matter what, she was revered and tasked with the great joy of becoming the mother to a Prophet. Maryam (Peace be upon her) was loved because of her purity and piety, and those lifted her above all other women to be chosen to carry Esa (Jesus) (Peace be upon him).

Maryam, who had left Jerusalem to birth Esa in the wilderness, returned to the city with the baby prophet in her arms. The people of the town were astounded to find Maryam holding a child. They asked about the baby's father, but Maryam had no answer. She simply pointed to the baby as ordered by Allah. The people asked how a child could hold the answers of his birth, that he was too young to even speak. Here a miracle of Allah happened! The infant prophet spoke to the people, telling of his birth and how he was born to a chaste mother. A pure and pious mother.

The lesson of this miraculous story is that even though Maryam (Peace be upon her) was faced with great ridicule and judgment from the people of Jerusalem, she remained silent and held fast to her faith. She knew she'd be returning to the city with an unexplained baby, but she kept her trust and faith in Allah. She knew that any fears she might have of possible humiliation and contempt would be nothing with Allah at her side. People may say hurtful things when they do not have faith or cannot open their eyes to hope, but Maryam was unaffected by these. In addition, Maryam (Peace be upon her) realized how impossible her situation would be to explain to others. She understood that not everything had to make clear sense when in the presence of Allah but that he will take care of things. This removed her possible fears, and she was able to return home confident that she had done exactly what Allah had planned.

We simply cannot know for sure how things will work out or what Allah truly has planned for us, but we do know there is always a goodness to His ways. Maryam and Esa (may peace and blessings of Allah be upon them both) are the prime examples of this. They were the purest of all in their time, and because of Maryam's faith and trust in Allah, she was honored and adored by having an entire chapter, (chapter 19: Surah Maryam) of the Quran named after her.

Prophet Esa (Jesus), Son of Maryam (Mary), Peace Be upon Them Both

Prophet Esa (Jesus) (Peace be upon him), one of the greatest messengers of Allah, was miraculously born without a father and spoke from the cradle. When he reached adulthood with a plethora of followers, He spread word of generosity, kindness, and Allah's message, but some in the Roman Empire felt threatened. The Romans tortured Esa (Peace be upon him) for trying to dissuade the masses from continuing their idol worship. They arrested Esa , persecuted him, and led them to the enclosure where he was. The Quran says at that point, before they could kill Esa (Peace be upon him), Allah raised him up with his body and soul to the heavens in a miraculous way just as he was born in a miraculous way. He was raised the same way and still alive and will come back close to the hour.

"And [for] their saying:

"Indeed, we have killed the Messiah, Jesus, the son of Mary, the messenger of Allah." And they did not kill him, nor did they crucify him; but [another] was made to resemble him to them. And indeed, those who differ over it are in doubt about it. They have no knowledge of it except the following assumption. And they did not kill him, for certain." (Quran 4:157)

The lesson of this story is that nothing is impossible with Allah. He is the ultimate protector. It is always wise to stay on the side of truth even if you are in the few. Have complete trust in Him.

Prophet Muhammad (Peace be upon him), the Last and Final Messenger of Allah

Now I want you to imagine the pain of the worst day of the Last Prophet's life, who was sent as a mercy to the whole universe and was the seal of the Prophets and Messengers. It was a time for great faith. He'd traveled out to Ta'if, a place fifty miles southeast of Makkah. The trek was difficult, but the heaviest struggle our Prophet faced was in convincing the masses that Allah was the one true God.

He had to walk through a narrow area without room to hide or find refuge. People threw things at his body and face, humiliating him and making him feel frightened. Not only did he face the internal pain of being isolated from his community, but he also felt horrible physical pain as the onlookers spat at him, punched him, and insulted him. He had but one companion, Zaid Ibn Harith (May Allah be pleased with him). Together, they walked and walked to spread Allah's message, but the people were unkind. They forced the Prophet and his companion out of the city. They endured being pummeled by stones until their feet bled and their bodies ached. The humiliation they felt for standing up for their faith in Allah washed over them. They were alone in their beliefs then, but they never faltered in their hope and trust for Allah.

The men walked around for eight kilometers in a state of trauma. Imagine the shock they had at what had happened; how could anyone dispute the love and strength of the one God, Allah? Finding a resting spot outside the city of Ta'if, they discovered a garden of lush greenery. They rested beneath the trees as our beloved Prophet (Peace and blessings of Allah be upon him) spoke to Allah.

"O Allah! To You alone I complain of my helplessness, the paucity of my resources and my insignificance before mankind. You are the most Merciful of the merciful. You are the Lord of the helpless and the weak, O Lord of mine! Into whose hands would You abandon me: into the hands of an unsympathetic distant relative who would sullenly frown at me, or to the enemy who has been given control over my affairs? But if Your wrath does not fall on me, there is nothing for me to worry about. I seek protection in the light of Your Countenance, which illuminates the heavens and dispels darkness, and which controls all affairs in this world as well as in the Hereafter. May it never be that I should incur Your wrath, or that You should be wrathful to me. And there is no power nor resource, but Yours alone."

Once again, I want you to feel how our beloved Prophet (Peace be upon him) must have felt and how beautiful his connection was with Allah when he felt sad. Remember, Dua (Supplication) is the tool of a believer.

Battle of Badr

For the Prophet Muhammad's (Peace be upon him) mission, the Battle of Badr was an important turning point for Islam. There were constant conflicts in Western Arabia during these early days, with polytheists and Muslims in endless battle. Our Prophet (Peace be upon him) fought for his faith and stayed true to Allah, even when most people would have given up or felt doubt. It took great courage and strength to achieve what he had, and it was all by looking past any anxieties that may have come from his epic quest as he held dear to his faith.

Now, the Battle of Badr is a landmark example of Islamic faith in history. In times of hardship, the divine power of intervention rings true. This battle saw three-hundred and thirteen Muslim soldiers under the command of Prophet Muhammad (peace and blessings of Allah be upon him) defeat over a thousand polytheistic soldiers. By Allah's decree, angels came from the heavens and helped the Muslims defeat the enemy. Our Prophet, assisted by Allah's divine intervention, used a single handful of dust to create a whirlwind that wiped out the opposing army.

"Remember when you cried for help from your Lord, He answered you. Indeed, I will aid you with a thousand of the angels in rows behind rows." (Quran 8:9)

On the eve of the battle, the beautiful Prophet, who was sent as a mercy to the whole universe, faced the Qiblah, (which is the direction of the Kaaba, the sacred building to which Muslims turn to pray) with outstretched hands as he began his supplication to Allah.

"O Allah, accomplish for me what You have promised to me. O Allah, bring about what You have promised to me. O Allah, if this small band of Muslims is destroyed, You will not be worshiped on this earth."

His supplication continued as he kept his arms outward to the Qiblah. His mantle fell from his shoulders, but he kept calling to Allah with his arms reaching. Abu Bakr as-Siddeeq, a trusted companion who was always near, came and placed Muhammad's mantle back on his shoulders. He embraced the Prophet, saying, *"Prophet of Allah, this prayer of yours to your Lord will suffice you, and He will fulfill for you what He has promised you."*

Ever wondered what he was worrying about? How dearly he loved his people and their future, and how he coped with his anxiety?

Through Duas (Supplications) and trust in Allah.

OTHER WAYS A MUSLIM CAN COPE WITH ANXIETY

When we give remembrance to a higher power, we are essentially thanking the One and Only for all His blessings and everything He has provided to make our lives so beautiful.

Treat your anxiety through the remembrance of Allah. This means to go out and be generous and forgiving and compassionate to others in your community as you remember all the wonderful things that Allah has provided. This includes his help in removing our stresses.

Abu Darda, may Allah be pleased with him, narrated that by repeating seven times in the morning and seven in the evening, *"Hasbiallah la illaha illahu 'alayhi tawakaltu wahuwa rabul 'arshil adheem,"* we are saying that *'Allah is sufficient, that there is no other god but Him, that we place our trust in Him, and that He is the Lord of the Mighty throne,'* Allah will remove the anxieties and stresses we feel. (Sunan Abu Dawood 5081)

This is akin to how affirmations are prescribed in other mental health books and guides. Here, we have not only the affirmation of positivity but also the faith and supplication to Allah.

Alter your expectations to suit your reality. Sometimes we are too harsh on ourselves and expect much more than we are capable of, which only puts stress on our minds and bodies. Be realistic and truthful to who you are and what you can handle.

Be the strong inner voice that you need. Tell yourself that what you are fearing is not real and does not have a place in your life. Only you know your deepest thoughts, and only you can silence them.

Practicing the principles of faith can make you feel fearless. Knowing that you are working in rhythm with the Almighty Allah and the Islamic teachings will give you strength in all your pursuits.

Do not compare yourself to others. When we begin to compare, we start to feel jealous and envious of the things we do not have. You must understand and accept the fact that there is always someone who will have more than you or be better at something than you, but that does not mean that you are the worst. You must only compare yourself to your own past triumphs and do everything you can to continue to better yourself with each passing day.

Take time to understand your anxiety. Sometimes we fear the things we do not understand, but by gaining knowledge, we gain power over our fears.

Work to improve your mental skills. Along with strengthening your brain through exercises that help enhance focus and problem-solving skills, you will also be removing the unwanted thoughts you may otherwise be struggling against.

Identify and pay attention to the triggers that are causing your anxiety. Knowing what is giving you grief can help you to avoid it, and this will also allow you to notice how much of your day you are spending focused on worrying about things that are out of your control. The quicker you become aware of how you are spending your time, the less likely you will take a downward spiral into that sea of worries that can feel impossible to escape.

Transform the way you feel and think in regard to your anxiety. By using the techniques outlined in this book, such as mindfulness and CBT, you can retrain your brain to think in a more positive manner, and it will help you to cope with your anxiety when it arises. These techniques will allow you to also live fully in the present moment and embrace your world as it is with acceptance and optimism.

Always hope for the very best but prepare yourself for the worst that may come. Use your faith and other techniques to build yourself up and remain positive as you face every obstacle in your way. But be honest about your position and remember what can happen if things do fall apart. This will allow you to identify what may come from your behaviors and prevent you from feeling depressed over failures, especially when they are out of your control.

Make Dua(Supplication) part of your everyday life. Dua is a weapon of faith. It is a prayer or supplication to Allah. Sometimes, we are unaware of everything Allah has done for us until we are put in an unfavorable position. In those moments, we cannot see the wonderful things we already have until they are gone. If we see this for what it is, for being without our means, our Asbaab, then we have no choice but to turn to Allah, al-Ahad. The One, the Only. He is all we truly need.

With Dua, we realize this and thank Allah for what we have. We even ask for help and guidance through Dua, noting that we are vulnerable and weak and rely on His strength and mercy. It often takes us time to realize the power of Dua, to know that we must trust in Allah with full certainty. He is absolute and sufficient, even in times when we are distracted by plentiful means (asbaab) or are lost and lonely by the lack of means (asbaab).

Allah is enough for us.

WHAT HAVE WE LEARNED

In this chapter, we have talked about how important faith can be in easing a person's anxiety and helping them to avoid feeling sad and depressed. Following are the key points that we have learned about faith and anxiety:

- Faith can provide us with meaning and purpose in our modern, chaotic lives.
- Having faith is to trust in Allah, the only One, with your heart and to be compassionate and hopeful for yourself and the people in your community.
- Faith can help us overcome our fears by realizing that we are not alone in our struggles, no matter how big or small they may seem.
- There are many ways that the Islamic faith can help a person overcome their fears and stresses. Of these, remembrance of Allah is highly important.
- Throughout history, various different Prophets and righteous people have experienced stress and anxiety, and Islam has helped to ease their burdens.

IN CONCLUSION

I must thank you for joining me on this emotional journey as we took a deeper look at stress and anxiety. As you go forth in your life, my wish for you is that you never feel alone or afraid in whatever situation you are dealing with, but instead, remember what I have said here and know that I'm with you, and together we can overcome these struggles.

There are so many amazing ways that you can help yourself to feel better from right this very moment. You can choose to be mindful and to look inside yourself to know who you truly are. You can step out and enjoy the sunshine and fresh air, stretching your legs and getting away from the burdens that are weighing you down. There are also nutrients and quality foods that can help you feel more like yourself, and those are things that can impact your life right now on this very day.

Do not forget that some struggles are bigger than we care to admit and that there is no shame in seeking out help for the things you fear and for the suffering you are experiencing. No one should ever have to feel as though they are broken or too far away from the light to find the goodness in their lives. There is always someone out there who believes in you and will fight for you and with you until you feel you've regained control over your life.

Finally, have faith in all your pursuits. Believe in yourself, believe in your goals, and believe in the higher power that is helping to guide you along every step of the way. Take solace in knowing that even when we feel as though we are walking alone, Almighty Allah is close.

Look back to these words often to find comfort and to ease your mind when it feels as though nothing may help. Remember what we have learned here together. Your worry is but a small part of who you are, and it is entirely normal to feel that way, even when sometimes it seems like it can be overwhelming. You are strong and beautiful, and I know that you will succeed and do anything you set your mind to.

Thank you for going on this journey with me. Trust always in yourself. You have experienced and survived a lot to get to this point.

You will continue to survive with your inner strength, positivity, and the commitment you have to the improvement of your mental health.

A GUIDE TO RISING ABOVE

If this book has in any way helped you along your journey, please consider leaving a brief review.

It is the greatest compliment to have someone spread the word of your hard work and to see the seeds of its conception begin to flourish.

As I have said, I want nothing more than to see you rise above your fears and live the life you've always dreamed of.

But just imagine how wonderful it would feel if you could help others do this as well.

In Islam, we believe that sharing goodness is a form of charity.

By sharing your thoughts, you're giving more than just words; you're giving a piece of your heart, illuminating the way for others.

With only a few moments of your time, your words could impact thousands of others who are wondering whether or not to read this book.

If you've found help here, please share that with someone and leave a review.

Thank you for your help.

The journey to overcoming challenges is kept alive when we pass on our wisdom – and you're helping me to do just that.

Scan the QR code to leave your review.

REFERENCES

"10 Famous People You'll Never Believe Have Anxiety," The Coaching Room, Assessed July 18, 2022, https://www.thecoachingroom.com.au/blog/10-famous-people-youll-never-believe-have-anxiety.

"10 Things You Should Know About Hijama Cupping Therapy," Seeker's Guidance, February 22, 2017, https://seekersguidance.org/articles/prophet-muhammad/hijama-cupping-therapy-sunnah/.

"Anxiety" American Psychological Association, Assessed July 9, 2022, https://www.apa.org/topics/anxiety.

"Brief Life Story of Prophet Nuh," Islamic Finder, Assessed August 16, 2022, https://www.islamicfinder.org/knowledge/biography/story-of-prophet-nuh/.

"Depression and Anxiety Self-assessment Quiz," National Health Services of the United Kingdom, Assessed July 28, 2022, https://www.nhs.uk/mental-health/self-help/guides-tools-and-activities/depression-anxiety-self-assessment-quiz/.

"Did you know? Cupping is actually an Islamic practice," The Express Tribune, August 18, 2016, https://tribune.com.pk/story/1163469/know-cupping-actually-islamic-practice.

"In the Belly of the Whale: The Story of Prophet Yunus," Islam Online, Assessed August 16, 2022, https://islamonline.net/en/the-story-of-prophet-yunus/ https://islamonline.net/en/the-story-of-prophet-yunus/.

"Isa (Jesus) - The Birth of Prophet Jesus (Isa)," Alim, Assessed August 16, 2022, https://www.alim.org/history/prophet-stories/29/2/.

"Mar 13, 624 CE: Battle of Badr," The National Geographic: Education, Assessed August 16, 2022, https://education.nationalgeographic.org/resource/battle-badr.

"The story of the Prophet Ibrahim," Human Appeal, August 24, 2017, https://humanappeal.org.uk/news/2017/08/the-story-of-the-prophet-ibrahim-as.

"What are Anxiety Disorders?" American Psychiatric Association, Assessed July 9, 2022, https://psychiatry.org/patients-families/anxiety-disorders/what-are-anxiety-disorders.

"What are Hadith?" Why Islam?, Assessed August 16, 2022, https://www.whyislam.org/prophet-muhammad/hadith/.

"What is the Sunnah?" Islam Online, Assessed August 16, 2022, https://islamonline.net/en/what-is-the-sunnah/.

"What is Anxiety and Depression?" Anxiety and Depression Association of America, Assessed July 9, 2022, https://adaa.org/understanding-anxiety.

Abusharif, Ibrahim N., "Learning from the story of - Magicians and Moses," Islam-City, March 11, 2015, https://www.islamicity.org/6520/learning-from-the-story-of-magicians-and-moses/.

Anxiety and Depression Association of America, "Anxiety Facts and Statistics," ADAA, Assessed July 29, 2022, https://adaa.org/understanding-anxiety/facts-statistics,

Astorino, Dominique Michelle, "What to Say to Someone with Anxiety, According to Mental Health Experts," Shape Magazine, April 13, 2022, https://www.shape.com/lifestyle/mind-and-body/mental-health/what-to-say-to-someone-with-anxiety.

Barnes, Kim, "I Have an Anxiety Disorder – Here Are 5 Ways I'm Coping With This Tumultuous Year," PopSugar, October 14, 2020, https://www.popsugar.com/fitness/how-im-managing-my-generalized-anxiety-disorder-in-2020-47779626.

Berry, Jennifer, and Perez, PharmD, MBA, BCGP, Alexandra, "Top 10 Evidence-Based Supplements for Anxiety," Medical News Today, May 22, 2022, https://www.medicalnewstoday.com/articles/325823#vitamin-d.

Browne, Ph. D., Dillon; and Legg, PhD, PsyD, Timothy; "Do Mental Health Chatbots Work?" Healthline, June 26, 2020, https://www.healthline.com/health/mental-health/chatbots-reviews.

Campano, Leah, "14 Celebrities Who Have Gotten Real About Their Struggles With Anxiety," Seventeen Magazine, May 18, 2022, https://www.seventeen.com/health/g40013141/celebrities-with-anxiety/.

Carmona, Melissa, and Williams, RN, Benjamin Caleb, "10 Best Vitamins and Supplements for Anxiety" The Recovery Village, May 25, 2022, https://www.therecoveryvillage.com/mental-health/anxiety/vitamins-for-anxiety/.

Cherney, Kristeen, and Legg, PhD, PsyD, Timothy J., "Effects of Anxiety on the Body" Healthline, August 25, 2020, https://www.healthline.com/health/anxiety/effects-on-body.

Clare, Tim, "My life was ruled by panic attacks. Here's my seven-point guide to tackling anxiety," The Guardian, May 22, 2022, https://www.theguardian.com/lifeandstyle/2022/may/22/my-life-was-ruled-by-panic-attacks-how-tim-clare-learned-to-cope-with-anxiety.

Coady, Serena, "Kendall Jenner Opens Up About Her Social Anxiety and How She Copes," Self Magazine, April 6, 2022, https://www.self.com/story/kendall-jenner-social-anxiety.

Dental Products Report, "Study finds more than 60 percent of people suffer from dental fear," September 13, 2018, https://www.dentalproductsreport.com/view/study-finds-more-60-percent-people-suffer-dental-fear.

Digital Editors, "David Beckham Admits Building Lego Sets Helps Calm His OCD," Cheat Sheet, June 16, 2022, https://www.cheatsheet.com/entertainment/david-beckham-admits-building-lego-sets-helps-calm-ocd.html/.

Elkin, Allen, "How Faith Helps You Cope with Stress," Dummies, December 29, 2021, https://www.dummies.com/article/body-mind-spirit/emotional-health-psychology/emotional-health/stress/how-faith-helps-you-cope-with-stress-163488/.

Etienne, Vanessa, "Gabrielle Union on Being a Rape Survivor: 'I Have Battled PTSD for 30 Years'," People Magazine, June 8, 2022, https://people.com/health/gabrielle-union-on-being-a-rape-survivor-i-have-battled-ptsd-for-30-years/.

Feintuch, Stacey, "Is Anxiety Ruining Your Sex Life?" HealthyWomen.Org, January 31, 2020, https://www.healthywomen.org/your-health/Sexual-Health/anxiety-ruining-your-sex-life.

Frank, DDS, Christine, and Higuera, Valencia, "Coping with Dental Anxiety," Healthline, April 15, 2021, https://www.healthline.com/health/anxiety/dental-anxiety#symptoms.

Glasofer, PhD., Deborah, R., "Best Apps for Anxiety," VeryWellMind, June 3, 2022, https://www.verywellmind.com/best-apps-for-anxiety-3575736.

Hendriksen, Ph. D., Ellen, "How Technology Makes Us Anxious," Psychology Today, March 27, 2018, https://www.psychologytoday.com/us/blog/how-be-yourself/201803/how-technology-makes-us-anxious.

HOLY QURAN REFERENCES:

https://quranonline.net/the-holy-quran/.

Al Quran-Surah Hud chapter 11, verse 45-47, https://quranonline.net/hud/.

Al Quran-Surah Al-Anbiyaa' chapter 21, verse 87, https://quranonline.net/al-anbiya/.

Al Quran-Surah Ash-Shu'arah chapter 26, verse 61-67, https://quranonline.net/ash-shuara/.

Al Quran-Surah Nisa chapter 4, verse 157, https://quranonline.net/an-nisa/.

Al Quran-Surah Anfal chapter 8, verse 9, https://quranonline.net/al-anfal/.

Al Quran-Surah Al e Imran chapter 3, verse 173, https://quranonline.net/al-imran/.

HADITH REFERENCES:

Sunan Abu Dawood 5081

https://myislam.org/hasbiyallahu-la-ilaha-illa/.

Sahih Bukhari

Ibn Abbas Radi Allahu ta'ala anhuma's narration, https://myislam.org/hasbunal lahu/.

https://hadithoftheday.com/ibrahimpart2/#:~

Horton, Lindsey, "The Neuroscience Behind Our Words," Business Relationship Management Institute, August 8, 2019, https://brm.institute/neuroscience-behind-words/

https://www.usatoday.com/story/life/health-wellness/2022/05/31/carson-daly-today-show-mental-health-series-anxiety-the-voice/9906476002/.

Husain, Habeeba, "The Wife of Pharaoh," Why Islam, Assessed August 16, 2022, https://www.whyislam.org/islam/the-wife-of-pharaoh/.

Kelly, PhD., Owen, "What are Anxiety Disorders?" VeryWellMind, May 14, 2022, https://www.verywellmind.com/anxiety-disorder-2510539#toc-treatments.

Lifestyle Desk, 'See, absorb, identify, accept it': Manage anxiety with the '3-3-3 rule', The Indian Express, January 15, 2022, https://indianexpress.com/article/lifestyle/health/manage-anxiety-mental-health-3-3-3-rule-7647177/.

Lockett MS, Eleesha; Wilson, Ph.D., MSN, R.N., IBCLC, AHN-BC, Debra Rose, "8 Research-Backed Herbs to Try for Anxiety," Healthline, June 3, 2021, https://www.healthline.com/health/anxiety/herbs-for-anxiety#herbs-for-anxiety.

Marcin, Ashley; Hoshaw, Crystal; and Boyle D.Ac., M.S., L.Ac., Dipl. Ac., CYT, Kerry; "What Is Cupping Therapy?" Healthline, December 23, 2021, https://www.healthline.com/health/cupping-therapy#conditions.

Maxwell, Victoria, "Advice That Would Have Soothed My Anxiety," Psychology Today, June 12, 2022, https://www.psychologytoday.com/us/blog/crazy-life/202206/advice-would-have-soothed-my-anxiety.

McClintock, Kaitlyn, "From Better Immunity to Better Mood: The Little-Known Benefits of Vitamin D," August 8, 2022, https://thethirty.whowhatwear.com/benefits-of-vitamin-d.

Merchant, Sohail, "These Chatbots are Helping with Mental Health Right Now," Healthline, March 2, 2021, https://www.aimblog.io/2021/03/02/these-chatbots-are-helping-with-mental-health-right-now/.

Mujahid, Abdul Malik, "25 Tips & Dua for anxiety and stress," Sound Vision, Assessed August 16, 2022, y.

Omer, Spahic, "Prophet Muhammad's Anxieties," Islamicity, October 26, 2020, https://www.islamicity.org/64940/prophet-muhammads-anxieties/.

Picard, Caroline, and Krstic, Zee, "The 8 Best Apps for People With Anxiety,

According to Experts," Good Housekeeping, April 16, 2020, https://www.good
housekeeping.com/health/wellness/g27128259/best-anxiety-apps/.

Piertrangelo, Ann; Cirino, Erica; and Juby, PsyD, Bethany; Can Anxiety Be Cured?"
Healthline, March 15, 2022, https://www.healthline.com/health/anxiety/does-
anxiety-ever-go-away.

Quaglia, Sofia, "Your Smartphone May be Able to Detect Your Anxiety," VeryWell-
Mind, December 10, 2021, https://www.verywellhealth.com/anxiety-artificial-
intelligence-5212637.

Relig Health, J., "The Effect of an Islamic-Based Intervention on Depression and
Anxiety in Malaysia," National Library of Medicine, January 3, 2022, https://
www.ncbi.nlm.nih.gov/pmc/articles/PMC8722650/.

Rogers, Kristen, "After years of debilitating social anxiety, a special tool changed
my life," CNN, April 1, 2022, https://edition.cnn.com/2022/04/01/health/
social-anxiety-cognitive-behavioral-therapy-benefits-wellness/index.html.

Ryu, Jenna, "Carson Daly Says He's Suffered from Anxiety, Panic Attacks on 'The
Voice,'" USA Today, May 31, 2022.

Sarah, "The story of the birth of Prophet Jesus (Eesa) and his mother Maryam
(Mary)," IqraSense, Assessed August 16, 2022, https://www.iqrasense.com/
people-of-the-book/the-story-of-the-birth-of-prophet-jesus-eesa.html.

Smith, Jake, "Adele Reveals She Experienced the 'Most Terrifying Anxiety Attacks'
Amid Her Divorce," Yahoo Sports, November 15, 2021, https://sports.yahoo.
com/adele-reveals-she-experienced-most-195600833.html.

Star, PhD, Katharina, "The Benefits of Anxiety and Nervousness," VeryWellMind,
September 17, 2020, https://www.verywellmind.com/benefits-of-anxiety-
2584134.

Taylor, Chris "Vibration Meditation: The Gadget that Calms by Purring On You,"
Mashable, March 23, 2022, https://mashable.com/review/sensate-meditation-
vibrator.

The Editors, "The Next Frontier for Mental Health Support: VR and AI-Powered
Chatbots," SupChina, June 16, 2022, https://supchina.com/2022/06/16/the-
next-frontier-for-mental-health-support-vr-and-ai-powered-chatbots/.

Todd, Carolyn L., "5 Helpful Things to Say to a Friend Whose Anxiety Is Skyrock-
eting (and 3 to Avoid)," Self Magazine, June 29, 2018, https://www.self.com/
story/what-to-say-friend-with-anxiety.

University of Illinois, Chicago, "A 'Factory Reset' for the Brain May Cure Anxiety,
Drinking Behavior, Study Suggests," Science Daily, May 4, 2022, https://www.
sciencedaily.com/releases/2022/05/220504153619.htm.

V. Juliette, "20 'Harmless' Comments That Actually Hurt People With Anxiety," The
Mighty, February 15, 2018, https://themighty.com/topic/anxiety/harmful-
comments-said-to-people-with-anxiety.

Wilson, Mara; Wilder, Robyn; Cosslett, Rhiannon Lucy; and Adam, David; "'Anxiety is part of me': Mara Wilson and other anxious minds on how they cope," The Guardian, May 25, 2022, https://www.theguardian.com/lifeandstyle/2022/may/25/anxiety-is-part-of-me-mara-wilson-and-other-anxious-minds-on-how-they-cope.

Yetzer, Brandi, "Inside Madonna's Debilitating Fear of Thunder and Lightning," Cheat Sheet, November 2, 2021, https://www.cheatsheet.com/entertainment/inside-madonna-debilitating-fear-of-thunder-and-lightening.html/.